My Naked Truth about Breast Cancer and Being Single

Freda L. Mays

1st Edition
© 2015 Freda L. Mays

Published by

WERD Publishing
4630 South Kirkman Road
Suite 808
Orlando, Florida 32811

Edited by: Priscilla Hawkins
All art produced by Paris Wilson

All Bible verses were taken from the Holy Bible or the New International Version (NIV) unless otherwise stated.

Printed in the United States of America
ISBN: 0692303707
ISBN 13: 978-0692303702

This is dedicated to...

This book is dedicated to my Mother who has endured so much before, during and after this project and, as Maya Angelou says, "Still SHE RISE!" I love you Ma!

To my grandfather who was the best male role model any girl could ask for...Thank you Papa!

To my best friend Drew..."I'm trying to keep it moving Cover Girl!"

To my baby brother, Norvell Mays, who is battling stage four throat cancer..."Lil bro, we are both on a precarious journey, but we also know God has our backs. I will keep it moving, if you will."

To all my nieces and nephews...Thank you for the way you always support and love me...I LOVE YOU BACK!!!

And, to all the single girls who are doing your best to just *"Keep it Moving."*

Contents

Introduction

I don't profess to be a writer. I am merely a co-author of my life, hoping to leave positive imprints on the pages of others. *My Naked Truth about Breast Cancer and Being Single* is a glimpse of my journey as a single woman dealing with metastatic breast cancer. I've endured some dark times on this journey, but I've also been the beneficiary of so many blessings.

I want to speak directly and honestly to you about my personal experiences as I continue to navigate through good days and bad ones – as I deal with the FACT that I have breast cancer.

If you are a believer in God, you know the dark times are the moments when you get the chance to show God how much you truly trust Him. I'm not saying any of this is easy; but if you have any better ideas, I'm all ears.

This is a journey I didn't choose. But I hope you choose to travel it with me through each chapter in this book. I also encourage you to take the time to think about and answer the "Free Your Mind" discussion questions at the end of each chapter.

One of the reasons I wrote this book, is so other women experiencing cancer will know and be comforted by the fact we can share so much with each other. None of us has to go through this dark place alone. I also want to help you navigate this journey by telling you what I've found to be most helpful to me. Even if it seems unlikely to you right now, I want you to know you can still feel good in your own skin -- in spite of having breast cancer or having a mastectomy. While some feelings of depression are normal during this time, if you feel depressed and are having a hard time dealing with your health situation on a daily basis, please discuss these feelings with your doctor or someone you trust and seek help. You don't have to go through this journey alone.

CHAPTER ONE:
OMG! Are You Kidding Me?

OMG! Are You Kidding Me?

I am a little country girl from a small town called Madison Heights, Virginia. I grew up with four brothers and five sisters. To my knowledge, I have no family history of breast cancer. So you can imagine how shocked and dismayed I was to hear a doctor tell me in July 2008, "You have breast cancer."

"*What? Seriously?*" I said. After coming to grips with the news, the only thing I knew I had control over was how I planned to deal with it. When I was diagnosed, my family was devastated and scared, as most families would be at a time like that. We all went into prayer mode. This was something so brand-new to us all. And though I trusted I would make it through this, I didn't know what to expect. Would I need a mastectomy? Would I die sooner rather than later?

My best friend and colleague, Eula "Drew" Andrews used to always tell me, "Cry, scream, kick or pray, just stay away from the black hole" (be it depression, negativity or complacency). Believe me, there are some days that are so rough I want to scream out loud. But when those days turn into weeks and those weeks into months, you've fallen into the black hole, which is very hard to rebound from. If you notice your friends don't call you as often as they use to, it may be because now you're making them depressed each time they talk with you. That's a sure sign of "the black hole."

You've Got to Move

Though I was told I had breast cancer in July 2008; as I think back, this journey really began for me in 1999. That is when I moved from Orlando, Florida to Atlanta, Georgia to serve as a music business consultant on several projects. I never had any intention of staying in Atlanta more than a couple years. However, I also had no intention of ever moving back to Orlando; but God had other plans for me, both coming and going.

Business was booming when I moved to Atlanta in 1999. However, by 2001 when Drew decided to part ways with our biggest client, things began to go south. In December 2001, as I was getting out of bed one Saturday morning around 6:45, something dropped in my spirit so strong telling me to move back to Orlando. I said out loud, "Really? Really, God?"

Have you ever been so moved by something you felt God was trying to tell you? I was so overwhelmed. It was literally as if a spirit was attacking me and wouldn't let go until I gave up. In order to calm down and digest all of this, I rushed to put on my workout clothes and jumped on my treadmill to burn off the excess energy.

The next morning, my friend Joni Hawkins called me to ask if I wanted to go to church with her. I told her yes, because I really needed a word from God. After entering the church and locating some seats, Joni said, "I'll be back. I'm going to get the tapes from the last two weeks' sermons." She and I had both missed church the two weeks before. Joni returned with both sermons, each with a different title. She chose one and handed me the other. The title of the sermon I had was "Leaving for the right reasons." *OMG!* I thought. *OK, God, I hear you.*

Have you ever heard the old gospel song, *"You've Got to Move?"* It begins with the words, "You've got to move" sang four times; and then the chorus states, "When the Lord gets ready; you've got to move, you've got to move, you've got to move." I understood. And I still have the cassette of that sermon to this day – yes, I said cassette!

After church, I returned home and started packing the very same day. It took me five days to get up enough nerve to tell Drew I was leaving. I wanted to stay just as much as Drew wanted me to; but she was dealing with some issues of her own that she needed to sort out without me being there.

I moved on December 30, 2001. I wanted to start my New Year in Orlando. When I moved back to Orlando, I continued to work in the music business until 2003. That is when I realized I was no longer happy pursuing the independent journey of being self-employed. I needed a more stable source of income. I finally decided I needed to fall back on my Bachelor of Social Work degree until I could figure it all out.

My goal was to take a job for a year or two while devising a success plan to go back to my passion – the music business. I accepted a contract position with Goodwill Industries of Central Florida, and was told the contract might only last a year or two. This was perfect for me and my overall plan.

However, the contract went on for almost five years, ending June 30, 2008. Shortly before the contract expired, my boss offered me another position; but I declined it because I was excited to go back into business for myself.

Knowing my insurance would also end on June 30th, I scheduled every doctor's appointment I could think of, including a mammogram on my last day on the job. I had no worries. I felt I was in pretty good health with no known health issues. I worked out, and I took vitamins and supplements every day.

The morning after I had my mammogram, I left Orlando and drove to Atlanta to hang out and celebrate with my best friend Drew. Drew and I were partners in crime. Whenever we visited each other, we would stay up all night – catching up on the entertainment business, relationships, and health issues. We *always* found ourselves laughing until we cried about real-life stuff.

Drew was well-known in the music industry, and many of our industry friends affectionately called her "Lady Drew." She had been co-manager of the internationally famous groups Xscape and Arrested Development in the 1990s. She also managed former TLC choreographer, Devyne Stephens. Devyne later became CEO of Upfront Records, and worked with major artists such as P. Diddy, Usher, 50 Cents, Mary J. Blige, Ciara and R. Kelly. Devyne has also been crucial in the success of artists Akon and T-Pain; helping develop them into the superstars they are today. So Drew's scope and reach in the music industry was wide.

I arrived in Atlanta the evening of July 1st. Drew had been having her own health issues. She had just been outfitted the day before with a catheter, in preparation to begin dialysis. I was so caught up with what was going on with Drew, I didn't notice until later that night that I had missed two calls from my doctor's office, asking me to give them a call.

The next morning, I called my doctor's office as soon as it opened. I was shocked when the nurse delivered the news that I had breast cancer. Doctors don't usually deliver this kind of news over the phone; but I was out of town. I had also been going to this doctor for more than fifteen years, and we have developed an awesome friendship. The nurse explained, the results that came back from my mammogram is showing activity in one breast that looked like breast cancer. All I could say was *"Are you friggin' kidding me?"*

When I told Drew, she was as shocked as I was. I was a 49-year old African American woman with many sisters, aunts, my mother and grandmothers; and no known history of breast cancer anywhere in my family. How could I have breast cancer?

Drew and I spent a great deal of the day discussing this disturbing news. Now, just when I was there to be supportive of her health issues, I had a medical crisis of my own. Drew tried comforting me by telling me the doctor could be wrong. That thought also entered my mind; but I couldn't help thinking, "what if the doctor is right?

I called the doctor's office the next day to schedule a biopsy. It was set for the following week right after the Fourth of July weekend. I arrived back in Orlando the Sunday after the Fourth, and had my biopsy on Tuesday. The biopsy confirmed I had breast cancer. Now there was no chance the original diagnosis was a mistake. Now I needed to know what to do next.

I sat there quiet for a moment with a smile of disbelief; filled with so many emotions. My friend, Michelle Hines, was with me. I remember her reaching over to put her hand on my shoulder. She really didn't know what to say to me. But she took over the questions, asking the doctor about the next steps.

I would recommend that any time you are going to the doctor to get results of any kind, always take someone with you to ask the right questions and take notes for you. When results are unexpected or may cause great emotions, having someone else with you is always a good idea. They may "hear" what you may miss.

I was initially told I would only need a lumpectomy; which is the removal of the small lump/cancer from the breast, followed by radiation. I had a lumpectomy later that month, but I didn't get a chance to take radiation before I was handed more bad news.

American Cancer Society statistics and informative tips from the Author

According to the American Cancer Society, "White women are more likely to develop breast cancer than African-American women. However, in women under 45, breast cancer is more common in African-American women." I was first diagnosed six years ago at age 49 with stage 3 breast cancer. Overall, African American women are more likely to die of breast cancer than other races. Asian, Hispanic, and Native American women have a lower risk of developing and dying from breast cancer.

'Free your mind..."

Do you know if you have a family history of cancer?

_____

_____

_____

_____

_____

Would you know what to do if you were diagnosed with cancer?

_____

_____

_____

_____

_____

Make sure you choose the best oncologist and best surgeon you can find

_____

3 John 1:2
Dear friend, I pray that you may enjoy good health and that all may go well with you, even as your soul is getting along well.

CHAPTER TWO:

You Wanna Cut Off My What?

You Wanna Cut Off My What?

The lumpectomy was scheduled for the week after the biopsy. My mother flew in from Virginia to Orlando to be with me. She arrived on a Thursday, and the surgery was performed the next day.

It is customary for a doctor to follow-up with a patient within a week or so after a surgery. My doctor scheduled mine for the following Thursday. My mom and I arrived at the doctor's office around 10:45 a.m. for an 11:00 a.m. appointment. We waited in the lobby of the doctor's office about 20 minutes before the nurse called us back.

I didn't feel anxious about this appointment, until I noticed the nurse was walking us into the doctor's office instead of a patient room. The doctor entered the room as soon as my mom and I were seated. He began to explain that during surgery, he discovered cancer was not only in my breast, but was also present in four of the 27 lymph nodes taken from under my right arm.

Then, before I had time to consider what he'd just said, came more dreadful words no woman ever wants to hear, "We have to remove your breast. And, you will now not only need radiation, but also chemotherapy for about six months before receiving radiation."

That's when I knew my whole world as I knew it – was about to change! I was shocked and devastated, feeling as though I was having an out-of-body experience.

When I was initially diagnosed with cancer a few weeks before, I was surprised and dismayed; but I never felt depressed or that I wanted to cry. However, when I was told I needed a mastectomy, I cried for five days straight!

Now, not only do I have to deal with the fact the cancer is more aggressive than I was first told; but I also have to deal with the lost of my breast – a major assault to my womanhood.

I felt very bad for my mother, because all she could do was put her arms around me and let me cry. I remember going into the bathroom one evening to cry. I was crying so hard and so deep that I had to cover my mouth with my hand so my mom wouldn't hear me.

I couldn't and didn't want to do much talking to anyone. I couldn't compose myself long enough to talk without crying. My mom gave the bad news to the rest of our family. I told her I just couldn't do it. I was having such a tough time thinking about the loss of my breast. How could I even visualize having only one breast?

I remember texting Drew to break the news to her because I couldn't reach her by phone. Later that night when we finally spoke, she began to tell me what a soldier she thought I was, and how much she admired me.

Yet, Drew was the real soldier. She was now taking dialysis at home seven days a week. She had to physically connect herself to a machine by 11:00 every night in order to be done by seven the next morning so that she could work. Let it run a full eight hours through the night; and disconnect it when treatment was complete the next morning. And here she was trying to console and encourage me.

Once a doctor says you need a mastectomy, please do not feel pressured to go with the first recommendation. Always get a second opinion. In fact, I got a second and third opinion.

Also, always check with your insurance company to make sure they pay for second and third opinions. When choosing a surgeon, choose one whose specialty is breast cancer surgery. I went with the first doctor I was referred to for my first surgery, the lumpectomy. He was a very good general surgeon; but breast surgery was not his specialty. This doctor also kept pressuring me to get the surgery done as soon as possible – as if he had already spent the money.

Of course you want to get the cancer out as soon as possible; but in most cases, a few weeks to research your options and process what's really going on in your life can help you learn more and make more informed decisions.

After receiving the grim news that I needed a mastectomy, I took my time and got a second opinion. The recommendation was to do chemotherapy first, to shrink the tumor; then a mastectomy. Because this was such a defining moment in my life, I decided to get a third opinion at Moffitt Cancer Center in Tampa, Florida. The surgeon there told me it was possible to save my breast.

This was definitely music to my ears; though I was warned there was a 50/50 chance it might not work. The doctor explained that she would perform a partial mastectomy, which involves going into the breast to get clearer margins.

According to the surgeon, surgery would involve removing the tumor, tissue beyond the visible edge of the tumor, and part of my breast, in order to get all the cancer. This would make one breast a couple sizes smaller than the other one. However, a doctor will usually schedule another procedure for a later date to make both breasts look even again.

My friend, Annette Cruel, drove my Mom and me to Tampa for the partial mastectomy surgery in October 2008. The surgeon recommended that I take chemotherapy and radiation; which I refused. I had heard so many horrific things about chemo including horrible side effects and people dying from it. Though I don't think I would make the same decision today, my attitude at the time was if it was my time to leave this earth, then I trusted God enough to be okay with it.

I felt great after the surgery. I remember the day I was released from Moffitt Cancer Center with a drainage tube and bottle hanging from my chest. When I got back to Orlando, I went straight to my polling place to cast my vote for president. I wasn't about to miss my chance to vote for Barack Obama to become President of the United States. But I was very stiff, sore and praying no one bumped into or even touched me while I was standing in line to cast my vote.

Inaugurated, Now Initiated

Three months later, on January 20, 2009, I was scheduled to go back to the Moffitt Cancer Center for a scan to find out if the cancer was totally gone. A follow-up appointment with my surgeon was also scheduled for that day. I knew she would want to talk about my refusal to have chemotherapy and radiation.

Three of my friends had offered to drive me to Tampa, but I told each of them no. I wanted them to enjoy watching the Presidential Inauguration Day festivities on TV. Barack Obama had been elected President, and I wanted them to witness the first Black President of the United States being inaugurated.

My mom had called from her home in Virginia to ask if anyone was going with me to this appointment. I told her no. I told Mom and my friends not to worry. I assured them I was going to get some good results and would be home in a couple hours.

I had been sitting in the doctor's office for about fifteen minutes before my doctor walked in. I did not like the look on her face when she entered.

First, she told me she was a little bothered by the fact that I, or anyone else, would refuse chemotherapy and radiation treatments. But in my case, she said, she was happy I had refused because not only was the old cancer growing again; but there was evidence of a new cancer as well. This meant I needed another surgery. This time, total removal of my breast was required.

As I sat there hearing this new diagnosis, I was overwhelmed and numb. I started to cry. And I had no one there to console me. I'd told all my friends I could handle this alone. I was wrong. This time I was crying because I knew I was out of choices. Now, I had to face what I thought I had previously avoided.

My mom was aware of the time of my appointment. I knew she was anxiously waiting by her phone in Virginia for me to call with good news. As I cried, I kept repeating out loud, "How do I tell my mother? I just can't, I just can't!" She was already dealing with my baby brother, who was diagnosed with throat cancer less than a year before. My surgeon, who had met my mother during the previous surgery, asked if I wanted her to call my mom; and she did.

The good news, my doctor explained to my mother and me, was that refusing radiation treatment actually had worked to my advantage. If I had gone through radiation, the doctor stated, this new surgery would not be possible. And as I look back on this experience, I realize my decision to refuse chemo and radiation treatments actually saved my life. I don't believe I would be here now sharing my story with you if I had made a different decision. Again, God has been so good to me on this journey. He has saved me so many times and in so many ways.

I dreaded the drive home alone. Then I remembered I wouldn't be alone. I prayed all the way home from Tampa back to Orlando. I asked God for the strength and guidance to make it on this journey. After arriving home, I turned on the TV to watch the remainder of the Presidential Inauguration Day festivities.

Friends and family started to call as they learned the results of my follow-up appointment in Tampa. I explained to them that the old cancer had returned; and there was a new cancer growing in my breast. Because of this new diagnosis, I would now need to have my breast removed.

None of my friends knew what to say. Not even Drew; but I understood. What can you say? I cried on-and-off through-out the day. I was so afraid, but I couldn't put my finger on the one thing that scared me the most.

I remember sitting up in bed that night around eleven thirty praying to God. "Lord, You said You would not give me more than I can bear—well, this is a bit much! My heart is so very, very heavy. How am I supposed to sleep tonight?" Well, let me tell you, I went to sleep and slept better than I had in years!

My eyes popped opened the next morning like a little kid's on Christmas morning. I felt like God was sitting on the edge of my bed just waiting for me to open my eyes to say to me, "If you trust Me, act like it!" From that day on, I've been free. I won't say I have never or will never cry again about the happenings on this journey, but I will say God has and always will have my back. I couldn't wait to call my mom the next morning to let her know that I knew I would be OK.

The tumor was inside the center of my breast behind the nipple. The doctors had to really dig into my breast on several occasions prior to surgery to feel the tumor. This invasive digging eventually caused my breast to hurt until it was removed three weeks later.

I had a total and final mastectomy on February 17, 2009. I remember waking up around 4:00 that morning, sitting on the edge of my bed just processing everything that was about to take place within the next few hours. The main focus in the days leading up to this surgery was God. I had done so much praying and so much meditating until by this time, I had accepted and was at peace with what needed to be done.

My friend Hope Bryant, "Hopey Dopey" as I lovingly call her, picked my mom and me up at my place around 5:00 on that Friday morning in order to arrive at Moffitt by 6:30. We arrived around 6:15, and I was prepped and ready for surgery before 7:30

I remember when the anesthesia was administered I tried to fight off the sleep because I knew once I woke up it would truly be a new day. But I also knew that no matter what happened; no matter how many tears I had to shed on this journey; God would still have my back. I knew it was only by the grace of God I still lived...and because He lives, I can face any tomorrows to come.

I woke up a few hours later still in good spirits. At least that's what my mother and Hope told me. I only remember the burning urge to see my chest where my breast used to be. I could tell that Mom and Hope were also anticipating my first look after such an invasive surgery. I still have the picture of me taking that first look that Hope snapped with her phone. I was relieved and pleasantly surprised it didn't look gruesome or spooky as I had anticipated. I had pulled up so many pictures from the internet of other women who had mastectomies; but none compared to my own experience. You can look at as many pictures as you want of other peoples' journeys, but none will be exactly like yours.

I was released from the hospital two days later with a tube and drainage bottle hanging from my chest. A follow-up appointment was scheduled for the following week. And, believe me, this time I took the nasty old chemo for about six months; followed by approximately 35 rounds of radiation, five days a week.

The first chemo made me so sick, that at times I felt being dead had to be better. I had refused chemo the first time it was recommended because I'd heard about the terrible side effects that can last a lifetime; but I was praying the benefits outweighed the risks.

I have neuropathy in my toes from that first round of chemo; and with each chemo after that, it has gotten worse. For more than 4 years now, in order to sleep at night I have to either take a pain pill or sleep with a heating pad wrapped around my feet every night.

The first week after the removal of my breast was probably the worse. I didn't want to constantly look at my chest; but I was forced to at least twice a day when my Mom had to clean and re-bandage my wounds. I don't know what bothered me the most – my breast not being there; my wounds; or the hurt and sorrow I saw on my Mom's face. She had to see her child go through some horrible things; and she felt helpless along the way.

Things were so rough until at times, I had to look in the mirror and get in my own face to say, "Look, if we're going to get through this, we have to do it together. You said you trust God, and this is just another chance to prove it."

This entire journey has and still does blow my mind to pieces. *But,* God continues to blow my mind even more.

Ladies, because breast cancer usually has no symptoms in the early stages, the American Cancer Society suggests you get your recommended screenings in order to detect breast cancer at an early stage. According to Cancer.org, compared to other races, black women are not getting their recommended screenings.

I'm not sure of the reason for anyone else, but I neglected to get regular Mammogram screenings because I was ignorant to the facts about who this disease affects the most, which are African American women. I thought I was very diligent about my health, following through with annual physicals, gynecological exams, dental appointments, etc. but because breast cancer did not exist in my family, a mammogram was not a priority. I sometimes feel guilty I've brought so much suffering to my family. When breast cancer is detected early, the American Cancer Society and many doctors have said there is a higher percentage chance of surviving; and in some cases, surgery can be avoided. And so can death.

You also need to be totally in tuned to your body. If you notice changes anywhere in or around your breasts, I encourage you to call your doctor as soon as possible.

And men, you can also help us with this area. I know this doesn't sound very romantic or sexy, but if you are caressing a woman's breasts and feel something unusual, please let her know.

American Cancer Society statistics and informative tips from the Author

The American Cancer Society and Cancer.org indicate that, "one main lymph node area (the armpit or "axilla") and two secondary lymph node areas (the internal mammary and supraclavicular regions) filter the lymph fluid draining away from the breast area. Since the job of the lymph nodes is to filter out "bad guys" like cancer cells, this is a logical place to look for breast cancer cells that have escaped the original tumor and are trying to go elsewhere in the body. Cancer cells may also leave the breast through the bloodstream and bypass the lymph nodes. However, the presence ("node-positive") or absence ("node-negative") of cancer in the lymph nodes is one of the most important signposts your doctor will use to determine the best treatment for you.

Another purpose of lymph node dissection is to remove cancer that might be in the nodes. This is done, so the cancer can't grow further in the lymph node area or shed cells that could go elsewhere."

"Free your mind..."

What are your biggest fears concerning your health?

_____

_____

_____

_____

_____

How do you prepare for the emotional wars in your life?

_____

_____

_____

_____

_____

_____

Mathew 11:28
Come to me, all who labor and are heavy laden, and I will give you rest.

CHAPTER THREE:

No Pain, No Gain—Really?

No Pain, No Gain – Really?

Yippee, it's over forever! At least that's what I thought back in December 2009. I had completed my chemo treatments by October 2009 and radiation in December 2009. Thank God it was over – or so I thought.

My last treatment was December 3, 2009. I was so thankful and excited for all treatments to be done. I wanted to try to move toward as much normalcy as possible. Up until December 3, I was getting up at 5:00 a.m. every morning to arrive for radiation treatments by 7:00 a.m.; and getting to work by 8:00 a.m. Most days I was fatigued and nauseated. I felt bad all the time.

My job at the time was teaching employability skills training classes. I would often explain my situation to the class; asking them not to be alarmed if I gagged or threw up. I used my situation as a teachable moment about dealing with hardship while looking for or trying to work.

Though my treatments were over, I was still battling side effects from the chemo and radiation treatments. But I was so happy to be done with that part of the journey. It took more than six months before I began getting my energy back; and before my hair slowly grew back.

Once you've been diagnosed with cancer and go into remission, it is recommended that you have quarterly or bi-annual scans for a certain number of years to monitor whether cancer is growing again. I enjoyed my freedom from cancer and from treatments. I loved working out again and doing just about anything my heart desired.

I was slowly getting my mojo back when I went for a six month body scan, and AGAIN was handed more bad news. In February 2012, cancer had returned. Though it came back in my left lung this time, it was still considered breast cancer because it was the same type cancer I had in my breast.

Getting the news about cancer returning affected everyone else more than it affected me. My faith in God had grown so much at this point; and I felt no matter what, I would be okay.

I would be less than honest if I told you I didn't feel some fear; but it didn't overwhelm or shake me to my core the same way as the initial diagnosis or the news about the mastectomy did. Other than being concerned about losing my job, and what side effects I may have to endure, my head was in a good place. All I wanted to know was – what's the next step?

The Sisterhood of Sharing Pain

Drew and I were both dealing with serious health issues at the same dang time. When I called to tell her about the cancer coming back in my lung, the first thing she said was "Dang, Mays, can I have anything by myself?"

And as usual, we still found so much to crack up about. However, Drew was getting weaker, and I noticed she was coughing a lot. I begged her to go to the doctor, as I'm sure other friends did as well.

One night she became so weak she could barely walk or breathe. She called 911 and was immediately admitted to the hospital. She was eventually diagnosed with a rare form of pneumonia which caused the lining of her lungs to harden and made breathing very difficult for her. She seemed to be more concerned about me than she was for herself. However, I was very concerned about her.

The week after Drew was diagnosed with pneumonia and admitted to the hospital, I had to have a port put in my chest in preparation for chemotherapy. A port is a device that is implanted in a specific area of your body, used to administer chemo and IV (intraveneous) medications.

I have a PowerPort, which is implanted in the left side of my chest just above my breast. Though at times, my veins still have to be accessed instead of going through the port.

I told Drew I was coming to Atlanta to see her. She tried talking me out of it; telling me she would be okay. And I almost didn't go, until my friend Joni told me if I didn't go I might regret it. I still thank Joni every time I think about it.

My port was put in on a Friday. By the following Wednesday, Drew could barely communicate; so I got in my car the next morning and drove to Atlanta. Yes, just one week after getting a port implanted. I thought about the Bible verse that says ---

"Greater love has no one than this: that a man lay down his life for his friends." (John 15:13)

You're probably saying, "Driving? Why didn't she fly?" Well, I was flying until the police stopped me and asked what the heck I was doing. I told him about my friend's situation, and he just gave me a warning. He could have also given me a ticket for not wearing my seatbelt properly, but he didn't. I explained to him I'd just had minor surgery in preparation for chemo; and was suffering from a cracked rib on the same side from a car accident six weeks before. Again, he warned me that if I have an accident, I would be better off if the seatbelt was worn properly.

I took both pieces of advice. I put on my seatbelt, even though it was pressing on the port site. But, I made a cushion out of paper towels to put between the tender spot on my chest and the shoulder strap. Then I slowed my little self down. I just wanted to get to my girl, Drew! I wanted to be with my friend and support her through this difficult time she was experiencing.

I arrived in Atlanta on Thursday, May 3 around 3:00 p.m. When I arrived, Drew's family and friends allowed me all the time I wanted to spend alone with her. It was hard seeing my friend connected to all those machines. I remembered Drew telling me the week before that being on the CPAP machine was like holding her head out of a car window, with the car going 90 miles an hour. Not a pleasant vision. And certainly not a pleasant feeling.

First, I sat in silence just staring at Drew and praying. For more than 10 years, Drew and I had talked on the phone every Saturday morning; sometimes for five or six hours. Now here I sat, speechless. When I finally spoke, I said, "I'm here, Cover Girl. I know you can't believe this because I can't either. But guess what? No matter what happens, you are going to be fine."

In the past three years, Drew had made it through dialysis treatments, open-heart surgery and a kidney transplant. I had no worries about her making it through this. She was strong-minded and strong-willed. She had endured the loss of both her children – 21-year old daughter in 1988; and her son less than 20 years later in 2003, when he was only 38 years young.

Drew had been blessed enough to get a kidney donated from a young man she barely knew. A young man who dated one of Drew's friends (Patricia/Pat) promised to give Drew a kidney if she needed one. Though he only dated Pat about six months; about a year after their breakup, he still kept his word and became a kidney donor for Drew. (Thank you, "J". When you gave Drew your kidney, you gave each of her friends a gift as well).

I knew she had survived so much. But I didn't know if she heard or even understood what I was saying, because her head was turned away from me. I continued talking to her when, all of a sudden, she turned her head toward me. Then she began turning it back again, but seemed to quickly do a double-take and looked right at me. I smiled as my eyes filled with tears from happiness and pain. I later learned that Drew was more alert than I had first thought.

On Saturday, May 5, just before noon, we were informed by Drew's doctor that her condition was drastically declining. The hospital had decided to disconnect all the machines that were keeping Drew alive. Drew's family and a small number of friends were called to say their last goodbyes.

I was standing in the hallway by the elevators when a very close friend of Drew's arrived. She proceeded to walk to Drew's room, and I told our other friends I was going with her. I knew how close she and Drew were, and I was sure she was going to break down.

I walked with her to the room, but stood just outside the open door to allow her some privacy with Drew. This friend began crying and laid across Drew's chest, as she cried and called out Drew's name.

Drew and I often had conversations about what we wanted and didn't want if we were incapacitated or dying. One of the things Drew told me she did not want, was anyone throwing themselves on her and crying. So when this friend laid across Drew's chest, I didn't have to say a word. Drew shrugged her shoulder as if to say, "Get up off me with all that." I was just as startled as the friend.

The friend stood there a few more seconds, still shedding tears; and then proceeded to lay on Drew again. Again, Drew shrugged her shoulder for the friend to get off her. 'That's when I went closer to the bed and put my arm around the friend and asked her to walk with me. I felt good that I could at least honor this one wish of Drew's. Even if no one else knew it, I knew I was doing something Drew wanted done.

A couple of weeks before Drew was admitted to the hospital, I asked my mom if she would mind if I spent Mother's Day with Drew since she hadn't been feeling well. My mom loved Drew as much as I did, and said she wouldn't mind at all.

I had no idea Drew would pass away on May 6; which is my oldest sister Dallas' birthday. She was laid to rest on May 13, 2012 -- Mother's Day. That girl took a lot of my secrets to her grave; just as I will hers.

I spoke at Drew's home-going service. I'd cried so much about losing and missing her during the days before the service. The last time I remembered crying that much was in August 2001 when my grandfather died.

On the day of her service, it had to be Drew who kept me going. I had written so many things to say, but nothing flowed or felt natural – so I winged it a little and also told one of her favorite jokes. I wasn't well enough to go to the graveside service; and even if I could do it all over again, I still wouldn't go. It was hard enough seeing Drew lying in a casket. I couldn't bear to see her being lowered into the ground.

It still pains me so much that Drew is gone. But then I sometimes smile to myself when I think how Drew always loved being the first in our group to do everything. She and I had talked a lot about what was on the other side of death. And, about what we would do to try to contact each other when we passed on. Every time I hear a bird chirping late at night or see a red bird, I think about her. Every time I see the number 1109 I think about her because November 9 is the day her daughter passed; and the birth date of my baby sister Noel who also died many years ago.

Every time I hear Jamie Foxx's song, "I Wish You Were Here," I can still see Drew crying as we watched him perform it live on TV one night. It made her think of her deceased daughter and son. Now when I hear that song, "I *always* think about you, Drew!" And how I wish you were here. Another song Drew and I loved is R. Kelly's "I Wish." Those are the times I wish I could hear God saying, "Wish granted." But I already know she's with me; because I carry her in my heart.

There aren't many days that I don't think about my girl, Drew. My heart still aches because I miss her so much. I keep a picture of her on my bedroom dresser. The photo taken in 2002, is of Drew, her son Jay, our friend Joni and me. Though it still pains me to look at it sometimes, I feel better knowing it's there.

Drew and I were like Thelma and Louise, Bonnie and Clyde, Salt-n-Pepa. She was my "ride or die." I could always depend on Drew. Anyone who knew Drew would have bet his or her bank account that she would have lived forever.

Someone asked me if Drew's passing made me think about death more. It really does; especially when I get the flu or pneumonia. But I don't obsess over dying. I just live and love as hard as I can with each day God blesses me with.

I often find myself wanting to pick up the phone and call her to share all the good and bad in my life. I have saved phone messages from her that I still can't listen to just yet. I stay in touch with her brother, Chris Aberhart, and her niece, Taylor Aberhart. Taylor had just completed her senior year in high school when Drew passed; and enrolled in college later that year. Drew would be so proud of her.

I know the majority of this chapter is about Drew. That's because there aren't too many things that happened in my life between 1998 and 2012 that didn't involve Drew or that Drew didn't know about.

Tribute to My Friend

Drew and I met in 1998. At the time, I was manager for II D Xtreme, a Los Angeles-based R & B group. The group needed a good choreographer; and in my search for top-rated choreographers, Devyne Stephens' name kept popping up. His manager was listed as "Lady Drew," so I called her and we clicked instantly!

We spoke on the phone several times a week after that first conversation, before finally meeting three months later. I remember that first in-person meeting. I picked Drew up at Orlando International Airport. We were looking to make a restroom stop prior to leaving the airport. We were so busy running our mouths, as we had done for months over the phone; we didn't realize we had walked into the men's restroom by mistake.

Drew stopped just inside the door. I had the nerve to keep walking – that is until I saw a man standing at a urinal with his back to me. He looked over his shoulder at me as if to say, "Come on, lady. It's the men's room, for crying out loud!" Drew and I ran out like two little girls laughing until we cried.

Since Drew and I were both in the music business and I was single; she offered me a proposal to move to Atlanta in early 1999 to serve as a consultant to her company. The best part of the deal was free room and board; which meant living with Drew in her beautiful three-story home. When we lived together, we acted like college girls taking the world by storm!

Together, we got through so many losses, health issues and successes. She saw me through losing my grandfather in 2000; and my grandmother in 2001. I was with Drew at a doctor's appointment in 2006, when she was told she needed to start dialysis within the next year to eighteen months. When Drew lost her son in 2003, I stayed in Atlanta for two months afterwards to assist her in running her company while dealing with such an enormous lost.

She was with me when I got the initial phone call from my doctor telling me I may have breast cancer. And, though we often laughed at each other's pain, and coached each other through a few disasters, we never judged each other.

I co-wrote a song for Drew along with a great songwriter, Angel Renee. The name of the song is "Save Me a Seat in Heaven." It will be released sometime in the near future. Please stay tuned to for updates:

Facebook: Freda Mays
Website: Fredamays.com
Instagram: iamfredamays
Twitter: iamfredamays

Here are the Lyrics

Save Me a Seat in Heaven

© Angel Renee and Freda Mays

Tell me what the angels said, when they took you by your hand
What did the Lord say when He saw you
marching in. How beautiful you are.
From the earth I see your star. You are my
true friend. Our love will never end.
Save me a seat in heaven right next to you. We'll
laugh until we cry. Our love will never die.
Save me a seat in heaven right next to you. You
light the whole sky. Our love will never die.
It's hard to know you're gone still. Your spirit
feels so warm. But I know you're right at
Home, right where you belong. Can't believe they called your name.
Look at all the plans we made. Came and took their angel away.
Save me a seat in heaven right next to you. We'll
laugh until we cry. Our love will never die.
Save me a seat in heaven right next to you. You
light the whole sky. Our love will never die.
Save me a seat in heaven right next to you. We'll
laugh until we cry. Our love will never die.
Save me a seat in heaven right next to you. You
light the whole sky. Our love will never die.
I'll love you the most and still hold you close to my heart.
I'll love you the most and still hold you close to my heart.
Oh, save me a seat in heaven right next to you. We'll
laugh until we cry. Our love will never die.
Save me a seat in heaven right next to you. You
light the whole sky. Our love will never die.

Written by Angel Renee
Co-written by Freda L. Mays

"*Free your mind...*"

Do you know if you have a family history of cancer?

_____

_____

_____

_____

_____

Would you know what to do if diagnosed?

_____

_____

_____

_____

_____

Make sure you choose the best oncologist and best surgeon you can find.

_____

_____

_____

_____

_____

_____

John 1:2

Dear friend, I pray that you may enjoy good health and that all may go well with you, even as your soul is getting along well.

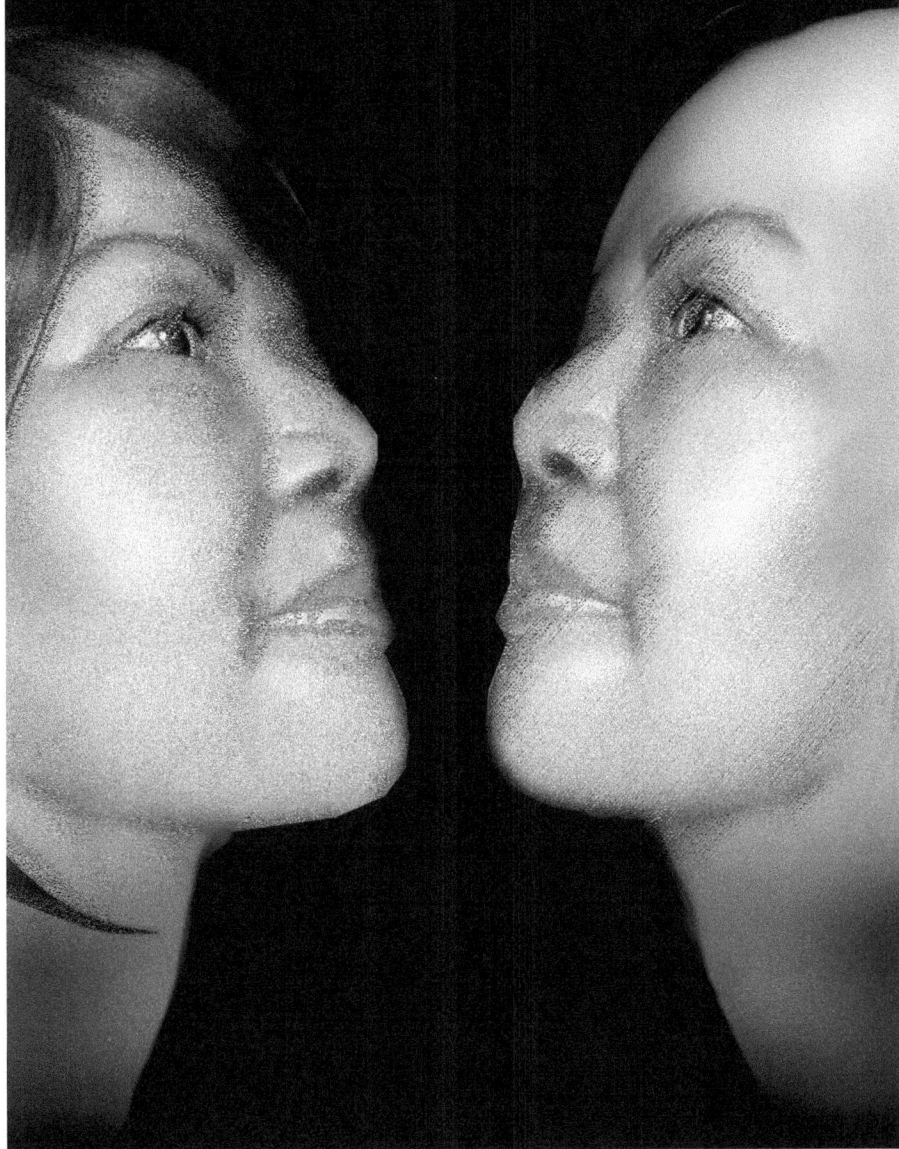

CHAPTER FOUR:
My Self, My Selfies!

My Self, My Selfies!

I'm still reasonably young (55 years old); so when the doctor first told me in 2008 I needed a mastectomy, I was devastated. I know this may sound vain or even crazy, but I think I had a harder time dealing with the mastectomy than I did the cancer.

So many things were going through my head. What would my breast look like? How am I supposed to deal with this from day to day? And though I wasn't in a relationship, I still had desires to be in one. Feeling good about my self-image after the mastectomy wasn't number one on my list, but it was close to the top.

Mastectomy and Reconstruction

After learning I needed a mastectomy, I asked my surgeon about having both breasts removed to reduce the risk of cancer returning. I also asked about breast reconstruction. I wanted both breasts to look the same. My surgeon explained it might not be the best decision for me, since I didn't have a family history of breast cancer. She also said most insurance companies won't pay for the procedures if they are not medically necessary.

I then asked if it was possible to save my nipple and re-attach it during reconstructive surgery. Breast reconstruction is a form of surgery usually done after a mastectomy to rebuild a breast. The surgery rebuilds the breast so that it is about the same size and shape as it was before; and looks as similar as possible to the other one.

Having your nipple and the dark area around the nipple (areola) reconstructed is optional; and is usually done three to four months after reconstructing the breast. This can take longer if your doctor feels the breast requires more healing time.

My doctor explained that reattaching my nipple was not a good idea because of the risk of cancer cells being present. The reason I wanted to save my nipple was to avoid having skin grafted from other areas of my body to form a nipple and areola. The other option would be to have a nipple tattooed on; but then it would have no feeling in it.

I wanted to preserve as much of the natural me as possible. Besides, I had no idea I would have to go through radiation and chemo first for about a year before I could even be considered for reconstructive surgery. Due to my current diagnosis, I am no longer a candidate for breast reconstruction because surgery of any kind could prove to be detrimental to my health.

Get Your Story Out There

A week or so after learning I needed a mastectomy, Lucille O'Neal, author of *Walk Like You Have Somewhere to Go*, (and mother of former NBA star Shaquille "Shaq" O'Neal), invited me to an event that included 30 to 40 people where I was asked to share my story. The event was focused on health issues that affect the African American community, including breast cancer. As I began telling my story out loud for the first time, I got choked up, and tears started falling like a fountain. It was amazing how telling my story for the first time affected me the way it did.

One of the best things that came from sharing my story was the way it touched others. A woman in her late 40s, who'd recently had reconstructive surgery, pulled me to the side after the event to ask what I feared most about losing my breast. I told her it was how my chest would look without my breast. I also wondered if I could have reconstruction, if the reconstructed breast would look very different from my other breast.

She asked if I wanted to see her reconstructed breast, and I said yes. We went into the ladies' room; she unbuttoned her blouse and pulled the right bra strap off her shoulder enough for her right breast to be completely exposed. I was surprised by how good her reconstructed breast looked; although the nipple had not yet been re-attached. She then asked me if I wanted to touch it. Now I know this may sound a little freaky, but I said yes. This boob felt normal. Nice and natural.

My curiosity was quieted; but I wish I had asked to see her other breast for comparison. I still didn't know how her reconstructed breast compared to her unaltered breast.

I know now that I needed to vent those tears that day. I felt safe and comfortable doing so at that moment. And it wasn't until then, that I realized I had been in mourning for the past week. I was grieving as though I was losing a friend. To many women, our breasts are our friends. (That's why we name them, right?).

I don't think about my breast a lot anymore until I'm changing my clothes, taking a shower or embracing someone. There have been times when I've left my house, am driving in the car and then panic, grabbing my chest to make sure I had the prosthetic on.

Just a couple of months ago, a UPS delivery man came to my door. I opened the door before realizing I didn't have the prosthetic on. I was hoping he didn't notice – but come on I'm a 44D – he noticed because he turned so red until I felt compelled to address the issue as I'm cracking the heck up on the inside. I politely apologized if I offended him in any way. He replied by saying something like, "Ma'am, I'm just doing my job," I'm sure he didn't know what else to say.

I would be lying if I said I didn't miss my *healthy* breast. But I often look at the scar where my breast once was as a war wound; and feel I won that round.

Some women choose not to have further surgeries. And some, like me (due to my diagnosis), are no longer candidates for more surgeries.

Though I was dismayed about the cancer and mastectomy, I trusted God totally and implicitly. I knew He would work all of this for my good. Crying didn't mean I did not trust God. I was trying to work my way through so many emotions as a breast cancer fighter and as a woman.

Mirror, Mirror! How I Like Me Now!

I'd always felt fairly secure about my self-image. I was avid about working out and eating healthy, and was always much aware of fashion trends. I once held positions as manager of a fitness center, an aerobics instructor, and then a personal trainer. I was confident about my body and how I presented myself.

After the mastectomy, it took about a year to feel good about my body again. However, other than a change in the style of blouses I wear; and not wearing open-toed shoes much; my fashion style hasn't changed a lot.

Since I'm a 44DD, I never showed much cleavage prior to the mastectomy, because it brought too much attention to my chest -- which made me feel I was sending the wrong message. Now, I have no cleavage.

Before the mastectomy, I could walk into any store that sold bras and buy some pretty, sexy bras with panties to match. After the mastectomy, I either have to order bras from certain vendors or do research to find out what department stores would alter bras for prosthesis to fit into them.

In 2010, approximately four months after completing radiation and chemotherapy, I began experiencing excruciating pain in my feet. Then I noticed the toenails on both my big toes had started to lift from the skin. My two big toenails were removed in early 2010 because they were affected by chemotherapy. This was the WORSE pain I'd ever experienced in my life! I would rather have my other breast removed than to ever go through that again.

Though they did grow back, my toenails are very, very sensitive. As a result of the numerous rounds of chemotherapy I endured, I now have neuropathy (a disease of the nervous system) in my toes.

I still love to wear the four and five inch heels, but only when I'm sure I won't be doing much walking. It's also difficult to wear open-toed shoes for long periods of time; because cool air causes my toes to hurt more.

Chemotherapy treatments also affected my fingernails. All my nails turned completely black and had stinky fluids oozing from them. They were hurting every day. To disguise the damage, I began wearing black nail polish every day for about a year.

Over the past year, I've gone from a size 10 to a size six because the treatments affect my appetite. I've had friends who've asked me to stop complaining because there are many women trying to get to a size six; and I understand that; but I'm not one of them.

I know some of you are probably wondering why this is an issue for me. I feel that if I get seriously ill, my body has a better chance of fighting if I have just a little more meat on my bones. However, do keep in mind that being overweight or obese is never good.

Hair Loss and Wearing Wigs to Cope

I lost my hair during my first chemotherapy treatments in 2009. I'd heard so many stories from women whose hair grew back better than it was before cancer; so I was excited at thoughts of how beautiful my hair would be when it grew back. Well, to my disappointment, I came out with the same hair I went in with; slightly curly and baby fine.

I like wearing natural-looking wigs. At one point, I loved the longer-style wigs, basic brown. Now I'm into the page boy or feathered look; not too long, but definitely not short. However, in another two months, my preferences may be totally different. I love the freedom and versatility of wearing wigs. I love the way different styles make me look totally different. However, I don't always wear a wig if I'm lounging at home or when I invite friends over.

Dealing with Hot Flashes—Times Two!

Hot flashes are a gift that most of us would prefer to give back. If you have or have had them, you know exactly what I mean. If you already get hot flashes, when chemotherapy is added, believe me, they magnify.

I remember making a quick trip to Home Depot one morning because I wanted to paint one of the walls in my dining area red. I usually carry a small fan and paper towels in my purse at all times because of hot flashes. But, because I was running in and coming right out, I only took my wallet and left my purse in the car.

As I entered the store, the worst doggone hot flash came over me. At the same time, I saw the cutest guy, who also noticed me as I entered the store. I went to a section far away from where he was and nowhere near the paint section -- hoping the flash would subside and praying hard that he wouldn't come to the aisle where I was. But, of course, he did.

By the time he got to me, the hot flash had decided to go into overdrive. Picture this – I was standing there sweating like a pig; wiping sweat from my face *with my hand!* I know, I know, but what would you have done? Needless to say, that was a short conversation. I was cracking up so hard on the inside; but believe me, hot flashes are no laughing matter when they are happening.

Of Course You Still Want Intimacy

Don't think for one minute that people with cancer do not still have intimate desires. Though we may have certain issues after a mastectomy, we still have emotions, wants and needs. We still want to be loved, touched and heard. Most of us still have times when we want to be intimate.

I told my gynecologist that if my vagina breaks, just shoot me and pull the plug. I know my mom and my pastor may read this book, but when you're on any journey that involves cancer, you try to hold on to anything that resembles normalcy.

A mastectomy affects different women in different ways. Some women avoid being intimate altogether because of feelings of insecurity about their bodies. A friend I've met on this journey told me that since she had her breast removed five years ago, she will not undress totally in front of her husband. She said unless the lights are out, she will not even be intimate with him. Because she knows how looking at where her breast used to be affects her; she fears it may affect him in a similar way, and lessen her husband's desire for her.

Her husband has tried reassuring her in every way that he loves her no matter what. I know some of you ladies are probably saying, "Heck, I turn the lights off every time too, and I still have both of mine!" And I understand that, too. Emotions and self-doubt can rattle the best of us in intimate circumstances.

Be Bold and Educate Others

I am an open book when it comes to my health. I've never had an issue sharing with anyone that I have breast cancer or one breast. Though I wasn't in a relationship at the time I was diagnosed, I've often wondered when and how women reveal to a date that they have one breast. I have now gotten to the point where if anyone wants to see my chest,

I show them. Most of them have said they thought it would look worse than it does.

In 2013, I joined a health group called Life Ambassadors 4 Health. We were a group of seven African American women who wanted to educate minority women; especially younger women, about being proactive about their health. We also held fund-raisers to support cancer research.

One weekend we decided to hold a retreat. We were having an informal breakfast meeting when I asked the other women if they had ever seen what a mastectomy looks like. They all said no; so I asked if anyone would be offended if I showed them.

I could tell that seeing my chest where my breast used to be had an effect on most of them. I later learned that some of them were surprised I had the courage to stand there and pull the prosthetic out. They asked if they could touch the prosthetic; and they then passed it around while I showed them my chest. No shame, no regrets;

I felt good, free and empowered to share this experience with my girls.

Men INCLUDED!

This journey can be frightening for any woman or man alike. Though the percentage is about one percent, men can get breast cancer as well as women. The American Cancer Society estimates the 2015 numbers for breast cancer in men in the United States are:

- About 2,350 new cases of invasive breast cancer will be diagnosed
- About 440 men will die from breast cancer

Breast cancer is about 100 times less common in men than women. For men, the lifetime risk of getting breast cancer is about 1 in 1,000. The number of breast cancer cases in men relative to the population has been fairly stable over the last 30 years. Famed actor Richard Roundtree, who played "*Shaft*" (in the 1971 movie) was diagnosed with breast cancer in 1993; and talked about it publicly five years after his diagnosis when he felt he was cancer free.

However, I want to say to our men, "Please don't leave us when we get the breast cancer diagnosis, especially when it results in a mastectomy. Having a breast removed can already have a major impact on our self-esteem; when you walk out on us, it's even more devastating."

"We need you desperately. Our children need you desperately. We are all afraid. I think most of us would stand by you if you lost a testicle! However, if you are more of a liability than an asset, it may hurt, but we will be so much better off in the long run without you on this journey."

Final Thoughts

Body image matters to a woman whether she's had a mastectomy or not. The more comfortable you are with your body, the more comfortable everyone else will be. Confidence is a secret weapon!

I can't say I'm in love with the scar on my chest; but I have totally accepted the fact that a boob had to die so I could live. Feeling sexy to me is a state of mind. No matter what you look like, carry it as if you're the most beautiful person in any room you enter. Then sit back and wait for the outside to catch up with the inside. It works for me!

American Cancer Society statistics and informative tips from the Author

History of Cancer, Genes and More

Having a history of breast cancer means your mother, grandmother, sister, or aunt has or had breast cancer in the past. Did you know that, "85 percent of breast cancers occur in women who have no family history of breast cancer?"

Cancer occurs as a result of mutations, or abnormal changes in the genes responsible for regulating the growth of cells and keeping them healthy. The genes are in each cell's nucleus, which acts as the "control room" of each cell. Normally, the cells in our bodies replace themselves through an orderly process of cell growth: healthy new cells take over as old ones die. But over time, mutations can "turn on" certain genes and "turn off" others in a cell. A changed cell gains the ability to keep dividing without control or order, producing more cells just like it and forming a tumor," according to the American Cancer Society.

FINGERNAILS / TOENAILS

According to The American Cancer Society, "Just as chemotherapy affects your hair because of the rapidly dividing hair follicle cells, it also affects your nails.

You may see a line in the nail related to the cycle of chemotherapy. This line is not permanent and grows out with the nail, usually in about six months. There may even be multiple lines and indentations reflecting the different cycles of chemotherapy.

Your nails may become pigmented or discolored. They may become more brittle, so they won't grow as long as they used to and may break more easily.

The area around the nail bed may become dry, and your cuticles may fray. Don't rip or peel off the loose cuticle. Cut it carefully with a CLEAN pair of nail scissors.

The nail may actually lift off the nail bed. While this, too, is reversible, you need to be very careful, for two reasons. First, the nail is more vulnerable and may fall off. Second, because the nail is not tightly bound to the nail bed, it can become a site for bacteria to enter. So be sure to practice excellent hygiene to avoid infection."

Weight & Obesity

According the American Cancer Society, "An estimated 1 out of every 3 cancer deaths in the United States is linked to excess body weight, poor nutrition, and/or physical inactivity. These factors are all related and may all contribute to cancer risk, but body weight seems to have the strongest evidence linking it to cancer. Excess body weight contributes to as many as 1 in 5 of all cancer-related deaths."

Losing a Body Part

Mastectomy is the removal of cancer, the breast, and some lymph nodes from under the arm.

Many women, married and single, have become depressed after being diagnosed with breast cancer; and then losing a breast – or two. I know some of you are probably saying, "It's not like you're losing a limb." But to some of us, it feels like it; at least in the beginning. And it is the loss of a body part; which can be traumatic.

Removal of a breast can add to a woman's feelings of unattractiveness. We are taught our breasts are a part of a woman's beauty and femininity. Breasts and nipples are also sources of sexual pleasure for many of us. They play a key role in women's sexual arousal and satisfaction.

Some of us also feel as though we've lost a limb. We become very self-conscious of how we will be viewed. And so, we have to invest in a new body part. If we don't want to freak people out or feel lopsided -- we have to wear a "breast form" or prosthesis (an artificial breast). This prosthesis is worn inside a bra to give the appearance and feel of a natural breast.

"*Free your mind...*"

How do you see yourself?

_____
_____
_____
_____
_____

How do you think others see you?

_____
_____
_____
_____
_____

_____

1 Peter 3:3-4

Do not let your adorning be external—the braiding of hair and the putting on of gold jewelry, or the clothing you wear— but let your adorning be the hidden person of the heart with the imperishable beauty of a gentle and quiet spirit, which in God's sight is very precious.

CHAPTER FIVE:
It's Aggressive, But So Am I!

It's Aggressive, But So Am I!

After the return of cancer to my lung in 2012, I was put on a drug called Herceptin along with another round of chemo. There are many forms of breast cancers. I have been diagnosed with what is called HER2+ breast cancer, which is considered aggressive because it multiplies and spreads rapidly. Herceptin, which is always given intravenously, is supposed to prevent the cancer from totally taking over my body.

I was told Herceptin can also damage the heart; and if combined with chemo, the chances of damage are greater.

In February 2013, after nine months of being on the combination, my heart was affected to the point where my ejection fraction (a measurement of the percentage of blood leaving the heart each time it contracts) had dropped to 43 percent, which was too close to heart failure.

My oncologist and cardiologist had no idea what to do at that point. The chemo was killing my heart; but without the chemo, I would surely die sooner rather than later. Hearing the cardiologist tell me there was nothing that could be done was a hopeless, devastating feeling. I left his office and sat in my car for a few seconds to digest and process what he'd told me. It was hard to swallow for about two minutes. But a couple minutes after getting this news, I said to myself, "I'm hungry! I've got to get something to eat," and went home.

For some reason I just couldn't receive what I was hearing. I wasn't in denial; I knew no matter what, I had to keep it moving. No matter what life brings I have to get up every morning and live life to the best of my ability. (See chapter ten, "Keep it Moving," to see more on how I keep it moving in my life).

A few weeks later, I was called in for an appointment with my oncologist. She told me she wanted to try something instead of doing nothing. She suggested I go on a chemo drug called Kadcyla combined with Herceptin. She explained that Kadcyla was a fairly new drug and combined with Herceptin might still affect my heart, but if I didn't at least try it, I would definitely not make it very long. I was administered this liquid form of chemo every three weeks and got scans every three months to monitor whether the chemo was effective and to gauge if the cancer was growing or not.

Three months later, my first scan showed no traces of cancer, which was very exciting news. My oncologist told me if I got two more scans showing no traces of cancer, they would end all chemo treatments; though I would still have to take the Herceptin.

The same month I started the Kadcyla, a friend approached me about a supplement that produced good results for others experiencing similar problems. So when my first scan showed no traces of cancer, I wasn't sure if it was the chemo, the supplement I was taking, or a combination of both. However, I would soon learn the truth. I believe in taking supplements if I can avoid taking more toxic medications. However, I always confer with my doctor before taking any form of supplements. Even when I wanted to try a new organic coffee, I checked with my oncologist first; to find out if there were ingredients in it that could counteract my chemotherapy treatments.

My second scan, in October 2013, also came back with no traces of cancer. I started celebrating and playing one of my favorite R. Kelly songs, "He Saved Me."

As a side note, a couple of years ago, I began planning my own birthday parties; celebrating with my "top-twenty" girls in Orlando, Florida. While celebrating at my January 2014 party, one of my friends, Debra Williams, gave me a beautiful frame with my Facebook profile picture in it. The frame has inscribed on it "No More Chemo 2014." All my friends and family were celebrating with me.

My third scan was planned for January 29; a few days after my 2014 birthday party. A follow-up appointment was scheduled with the oncologist for February 11. However, my oncologist called me the day after my scan to tell me the scan showed the cancer had now spread to three other areas in my body. This spreading of cancer cells is called metastatic breast cancer. It is also referred to as advanced breast cancer.

At this point I was numb and disappointed because I really felt I was finally on the right track – doing more of what would keep me moving in the right direction. I just knew I would beat it this time. What is going on with my body, I thought? What is God saying to me? I phoned my mom and could tell immediately that she was a little overwhelmed by the news. But as always, in the time of trouble her favorite line is, "God's got it."

I ended up in the hospital with pneumonia a few days after getting the news. This was the day before I was supposed to see the oncologist to discuss a treatment plan. Though I knew I was in bad medical condition, while lying in the hospital bed all I could think about was my girl Drew. She had gone in the hospital, diagnosed with pneumonia two years before and never made it out.

From her seat in heaven, I must have talked Drew's ear off while I was in the hospital. I said, "I miss you Cover Girl, and want you to save me a seat, but not quite yet."

I thought I was finally going to be freed of this disease; but to my amazement, it's gaining on me instead. And though I was shaken and confused, I didn't break.

I finally met with my oncologist a week after being released from the hospital. She came in the room, sat down, looked me in my eyes and told me the cancer had spread to six areas in my body -- stomach, spine, under my left arm, left front side rib, thyroid and in the lymph nodes surrounding my lungs -- instead of three as she originally thought. Again, I was shocked but not too overwhelmed. God and I had been down this road too many times for me freak out.

My friend, Joni Hawkins, was with me during this visit. When she heard this news from my doctor, her mouth dropped open and stayed opened so long it looked like she was holding a long musical note.

The good news was, there were now other new treatments I was a candidate for – though some were less than a year old. This time around I was given the option of taking chemo pills (Affintor and Aromasin) orally every day. Or I could choose to take the liquid chemo intravenously every three weeks when I took the Herceptin.

I asked my oncologist about the pros and cons of both options. She stated the only difference would be the side effects. Though it would only be administered every three weeks, she said the side effects from the liquid chemo would be more severe. I chose the pills in order to have a better quality of life; and because I was single, I needed to be able to continue working.

I started the new chemo pills in February 2014. So far, the only side effects I've experienced are minor itching, constipation, dry skin, stiff joints, occasional nausea, loss of appetite and fatigue. And again, the drug combination does affect my heart.

I was skeptical in the beginning about choosing to take the chemo orally every day, because I was afraid I might forget to take them sometime. But my life depends on it, for that reason I can remember. In the first few months though, I had to remember to take the chemo pills and a heart medication three times a day. So that I would not forget, I had to set the alarm on my phone to remind myself; and one of my goddaughters would text me every day to remind me. I don't regret choosing to take the oral form of this treatment.

I had my first scan from this round of chemo on May 20, 2014. Though it showed no traces of cancer, this time around my oncologist explained that it means the chemo is working.

As an African American woman diagnosed with breast cancer, I beg each of you to ALWAYS follow through with your recommended mammograms. I especially urge African American women to get genetic testing to find out if you carry the BRCA gene. We are dying much more than any other race, and being tested for this gene could help us make better choices before being diagnosed, in order to reduce our death rate.

A gene is a piece of DNA inside a cell that has the information to make a specific protein. The BRCA gene test is a blood test that uses DNA analysis to identify harmful changes (mutations) in either one of the two breasts cancer susceptibility genes — BRCA1 and BRCA2. The anonym BRCA is derived from the words BReast CAncer.

If you carry the BRCA gene, you have a higher percent risk of developing breast cancer and higher percent risk of developing ovarian cancer?

When you get tested, if you learn you carry this gene, you can be proactive just as actress Angelina Jolie was – if you choose. Her mother died from ovarian cancer. Jolie got tested; and learned she had the BRCA gene. She chose preventive surgery and had both breasts removed in 2013 to prevent breast cancer. Recent news stories have indicated she is also considering having her ovaries removed to prevent ovarian cancer.

I've also learned African Americans are less likely to participate in clinical trials than other groups; and I believe this may be another reason greater numbers of us are dying from cancer.

Prior to being diagnosed with breast cancer, I was skeptical about clinical trials of any kind, until I learned how just about any drug humans consume – including high blood pressure and heart disease drugs – had to go through a clinical trial first.

This is how my oncologist explained it to me. The drug is first tested in a lab, then on animals, and then humans. She also explained that unlike other trials, the placebo or "sugar pill" is never given in a clinical trial for any type of cancer. I was ready to participate in a clinical in 2014, but was offered to try the two drugs I'm currently on which have worked fairly well so far. But I constantly talk to my doctor about clinical trials, and urge my family and friends to participate when possible and beneficial.

American Cancer Society statistics and informative tips from the Author

African Americans, Genetic Testing and Clinical Trials

Please participate in any clinical trials you may be qualified for. Although we are more likely to die from breast cancer (and other cancers), African Americans are less likely to participate in clinical trials. Food for thought: Could this be one of the reasons we are dying more from cancer than other races. If we don't participate, they won't know exactly how to medically treat us. Do not depend on your doctors to keep you updated on the latest trials. Be proactive and ask your doctors.

Clinical trials, according to the American Cancer Society, are research studies that use human volunteers. The trials usually test new drugs or other treatments to compare current standard treatments with others that may be better. They may also test new ways to diagnose or prevent a disease. Before a new treatment or test is used on people, it is studied in the lab. If lab studies suggest it will work, the next step is to test it in patients. There are three main questions the researchers want to answer; (1) Does this treatment or test work better than what we use now? (2) What side effects does it cause? And (3) Do the benefits outweigh the risks? You can also learn more information by going to: clinicaltrials.gov

"*Free your mind...*"

How do you cope when dealt a bad hand in life?

_____

_____

_____

_____

_____

Do you really believe prayer can make a difference in your life?

_____

_____

_____

_____

_____

_____

Psalm 27:1
The LORD is my light and my salvation; whom shall I fear? The LORD is the strength of my life; of whom shall I be afraid?

CHAPTER SIX:

Goodwill = God's Will

Goodwill = God's Will

In 2008, had I not chosen to leave my job, I might not be here today to share my story. Remember, I only got a mammogram at that time because my job was ending; and my insurance ending with it. When I was diagnosed, I already had stage three cancer. Can you imagine where I would be if I had waited another year or two to have a mammogram? I can.

I returned to Goodwill Industries of Central Florida in August 2010 as the director of community and employment services. I was constantly in and out of the hospital, missing many days from work; using all my vacation and personal days. Unless I worked, I didn't get paid, which resulted in more funds going out than I had coming in.

However, in May 2014, I was thankful and humbled when one of my doctors cared enough to get in my face for a reality talk. She told me the form of breast cancer I had, the chemotherapy treatments, and working a full-time job – would kill me much sooner than later.

I exhaled – because I knew she was right when she told me I needed to think about giving up working full-time. I exhaled because I think I was just waiting for someone to shake me and say, "What are you doing?"

I think the hardest thing about giving up my job was the fact that I am single, and was unsure how I would support myself. Giving up a decent salary and decent benefits was hard. But I didn't want to be the person who is wheeled out on a stretcher from work; and never sees home again because I chose to work until I dropped.

I miss my Goodwill family and continue to stay in contact with many of them. I do know that if I hadn't left my job, I would not have made it much longer. My body feels so tired more times than not these days. I have missed out on so many events – birthday parties, family reunions, my baby brother's wedding, and so on – all because I chose to work full time and was either sick or too fatigued to travel or participate. However, I do not hold one ounce of regret. I met some of my "bestest" friends for life at Goodwill Industries of Central Florida, and I am humbled and thankful to God for it.

To this day, I know God kept bringing me back to Goodwill for many reasons. I told you He has to bang me upside my head several times in order for me to get a clue.

My doctor could only advise me, but I had to make the decision to leave or not leave my job. Though it took me three months to do it, I chose to leave and live a longer, healthier life on my feet. I realize I could die sooner rather than later, but I also realize I could outlive most of my family and friends, if it's God's will.

Leaving my job in August 2014 may not totally save my life; but hopefully it will give me more energy to enjoy the rest of it on my feet for a longer period of time. You see, I still have things on my bucket list to accomplish.

I know I keep saying it feels like I'm having an out-of-body experience; but that is exactly what it feels like to me. I am sitting back – waiting to see what happens next – as if I'm watching a movie.

I often ask my body, "How much longer are you going to hold up for me?" I am so glad this battle is not mine alone; it's the Lord's. So I am DETERMINED to live life as fully as possible until I die.

"*Free your mind...*"

Do you know your balance in life?

_____

_____

_____

_____

_____

Would you know when to quit something or someone?

_____

_____

_____

_____

_____

_____

Isaiah 43: 18-19
Remember not the former things, nor consider the things of old. Behold, I am doing a new thing; now it springs forth, do you not perceive it? I will make a way in the wilderness and rivers in the desert.

CHAPTER 7
Make a List and Check It Twice!

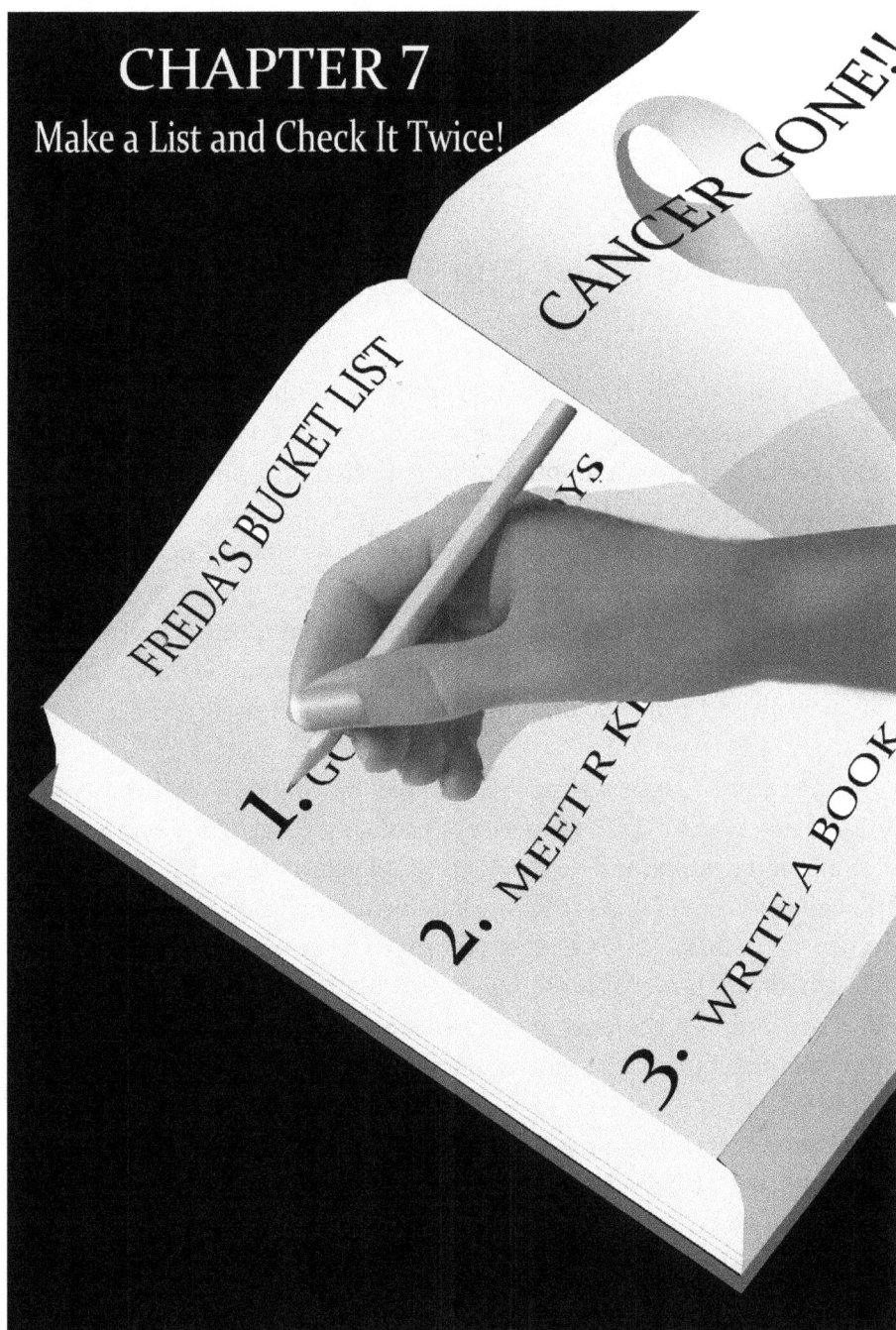

CANCER GONE!!

FREDA'S BUCKET LIST

1. GO ...YS

2. MEET R K...

3. WRITE A BOOK

Make a List and Check It Twice!

A bucket list -- which some prefer to call a life list -- is a list of things you hope to do before you die. But why do most of us wait until a doctor says we have a certain amount of time to live in order to start accomplishing things on our list?

I've been a goal setter and a dreamer ever since I can remember. I remember standing in the middle of my grandparent's corn fields when I was 11 or 12, watching as a plane flew above. I remember saying, one day I'll be on one of those planes because I'll own my own business. And I did – owning my first business shortly after college at 22 years old.

But I think the first time I remember writing down what I call my bucket list, was in 2003 after Drew's son Jay passed. Jay had so many dreams and desires; and he died at only 38 years young. I slowly accomplished some small feats from my list during the years after that. Then I refocused in 2012, when cancer returned in my lung. And though I felt like I had much more life in me, I couldn't ignore what was going on with my body. In the past a goal list always motivated me to succeed; now having a bucket list motivates me to live and realize more dreams while doing so.

There is no right or wrong way to compile a bucket list. I use to separate what I called my goal list from what I called my bucket list. Becoming more tech savvy is a goal. Meeting two of my all-time favorite music artists – those are bucket list items I can now check off my list!

BUCKET LIST – #1 (Before the cancer diagnosis)

I met 2PAC at the *Sunset Park* movie premiere in Los Angeles in March 1996; prior to his demise in September 1996. A group I managed at the time, the 69 Boyz, was on the *Sunset Park* soundtrack along with 2PAC. I even had the opportunity to have a conversation with 2PAC. I told him how much I admired him, and he said, "Thank you." That's considered a conversation, right? I also met Rosie Perez, who is another person I've always admired for her craft of great acting.

The picture the 69 Boyz and I took with 2PAC has been on my wall for more than ten years. I also have a gigantic Vibe Magazine 1996 commemorative poster of him -- framed and hanging on my dining room wall. I can still remember standing beside him as if it was last year. R.I.P. PAC.

BUCKET LIST – #2 (After the cancer diagnosis)

Devyne Stephens, who I mentioned in Chapter One, and another great friend, Wayne "Big Wheezy" Stallings, found out that meeting R. Kelly was on my bucket list – and just like that – I was in Atlanta. Devyne had been working with R. Kelly in Atlanta on and off for more than four months in preparation for an upcoming tour set to begin April 2014.

Wayne called me one evening after learning about my recent cancer diagnosis from another friend. During this conversation, I told Wayne that meeting (singer/songwriter) R. Kelly was on my bucket list. He asked when I wanted to come to Atlanta; and I told him within the next two or three weeks. He said okay. Then he phoned me a couple days later to say if I wanted to meet R. Kelly, I would need to be in Atlanta by the weekend – in three days. Kelly, he said, would be leaving for Chicago on Monday to prepare for his upcoming tour.

Now I'm really freaking out a little because of the short notice, and because this will be my first trip back to Atlanta since Drew passed. However, Devyne helped relieve some of the anxiety by taking care of all the accommodations.

It had been less than a month since I returned to work from the hospital. Knowing that my supervisor would be concerned about my health, I was reluctant to ask for time off. And though she gave me the "Mother" look, she knew this was a bucket-list item and reluctantly, but happily said yes. I was so excited I had to tell everyone I met; people at work, the doctor's office, and even at the grocery store knew I was going to meet R. Kelly.

I arrived in Atlanta and checked into my hotel Friday around noon. Though I really wanted to hang out with a couple of my friends on Friday night, I stayed in due to fatigue from treatments the week before. There was no date or time set to meet Kelly so I was sort of on an on-call status.

I waited and waited and waited. I filled my time shopping with a friend on Saturday; though Devyne's assistant kept updating me. By midnight when I went to bed, I still had not received the call to come to the studio. Now I thought, after all of my excitement, anticipation and bragging, I would go back to Orlando heartbroken and humiliated. But at 1:15 a.m., Wayne called and asked if it was too late for me to come out. Late, yes. Tired, yes. Overstressed, yes. But you better believe I got up and got dressed. Not in the new clothes I'd bought; but in the same clothes I'd worn on the plane.

When we arrived at Devyne's house around 1:45 a.m., Kelly was already there, but not in the room I initially entered. I was there about 20 minutes before Devyne walked Kelly into the room to meet me. As Devyne introduced me to R. Kelly, I stretched my hand to shake his. Instead, he smiled and said, "Give me a hug." That put me at ease and I exhaled a little. However, I was a little concerned when hugging him. I never know what the prosthetic breast I wear feels like to people I hug. But I quickly forgot about that when I realized I was "I was chilling with the King of R & B," Mr. R. Kelly.

My friend Paris Wilson, an artist, had prepared a painting of R. Kelly for me especially for this trip. Before showing the painting, I told R. Kelly if he didn't approve of it and didn't want to autograph it, I would understand. As a former personal manager in the music business, I often advised performers not to do anything that did not support their image in the business, so I understood he might be hesitate to sign it.

When I pulled the painting out of the tube, I saw by his reaction he liked it. Then he said, "Before I write on this, where is my copy?" I told him I would send him a copy -- "but this one was mine." I was supposed to give him his copy when attending his concert in Tampa or Jacksonville, Florida within the following weeks but was unable to because I was sick. I will make sure he gets it somehow.

R. Kelly was so down-to-earth, so cool, all I expected and more. He took time to show me love even though he was preparing for a tour the following week. I pray for him whenever I think about him; dude has so much in mind and in his heart. "Prayer changes things, ROB."

BUCKET LIST – #3

A few weeks after returning from Atlanta, hanging out with R. Kelly, I wanted to share my joy with my friends and family by posting it on Facebook. I also posted that the next thing on my bucket list was to tour the new Dallas Cowboys stadium and go to a game. And I told my sister Polly, who is a die-hard Redskins fan, not to respond with any snide comments.

My mom came to visit me in early May 2014 to attend a charity event produced by Lucille O'Neal. I had some cancer complications and ended up in the hospital, so my mom extended her stay.

On Mother's Day, my sister Polly called to wish our mom a Happy Mother's Day. I walked into the bedroom while they were on the phone, and Polly asked to speak to me. Instead of handing me the phone, my mom put it on speaker saying, "You know I'm a little nosey."

"I've got a comeback to your Facebook post," Polly said. "Pack your bags and book the tickets because you and a friend are going to see a Dallas Cowboys game and tour the new stadium!"

I don't have any kids, but I started doing the happy dance, saying, "This is the best Mother's Day ever!"

Unfortunately, due to 2014 being such a rough year for me health wise, I haven't been able to take this trip. If God is willing, I'm very hopeful to take this trip during the 2015-2016 season and hope to see Dallas go to the Super Bowl.

BUCKET LIST – #4

Writing a book has been on my bucket list for many years. I wrote a book some years ago called *Music Business Terms and More (with contributions by Entertainment Attorney Gary Greenberg)*. It was never published; but will be my second release following this one. For right now, thank God, *My Naked Truth about Breast Cancer and Being Single* is born.

The primary reason for writing this book was to document this journey for my family, friends and other loved ones.

And as I stated earlier, I also want other women experiencing stage 4 cancer or similar journeys to know and be comforted by the fact that we can share so much with each other.

BUCKET LIST – #5

Another thing on my bucket list is to do a ten-minute stand-up routine about single women and breast cancer. I've tried some of my material on my friends. And now, I'd love to share one joke with you, so here goes:

TITLE OF JOKE: Did He Eat the WHOLE Thing
© Freda Mays, October 2014

After being away from the dating scene a long time, the question I kept asking myself was, when do you tell your date you only have one breast? I had been dating this guy for a couple months and had not yet told him I only have one breast. One Friday night this dude came over to my place looking so fine; but I noticed either he had been smoking something or was very sleepy because his eyes were squinted to the point he looked Asian. But it didn't matter to me because he looked so dang fine! The lights were dimmed, candles were lit, and one thing led to another...I thought everything was going well without me telling him about my missing breast, until he abruptly stopped, grabbed his clothes, and ran out!

He called me the next morning, and I said, "Hey Tyrone, what happened last night? Why did you run out like that? Are you OK?"

He said, "Um, when I came to your place last night did you have two breasts?" This silly boy had the munchies and thought he ate one of my breasts!

By no means do I want to be a comedian. Humor has gotten me over many hills and mountains. Every day I rise, I pray I can put a smile on someone's face or a healthy laugh in someone's heart.

BUCKET LIST – # 6

While thinking about my legacy, setting up a college fund for my nieces and nephews has always been a goal and now one of my most passionate bucket list items; the majority of the funds from this book will go towards that fund.

Other bucket list items include:

- Traveling to Dubai
- Going to Jerusalem. I don't know how but I'm currently working on my passport..."Faith without works is DEAD!"
- Meeting Mark Cuban
- Going to Las Vegas taking at least five of my friends
- Building my mom her dream house
- Producing a musical stage play
- Going to the Grand Canyons
- Stamping out cancer!!!

No matter what happens, as long as I have breath in my body, I will always reach for the stars and accomplish all I can on my list!

"I can do all things through Christ who strengthens me." **Philippians 4:13**

Call it your bucket list or life list. Either way, it's the things you want to do while you occupy your space in this world. As the Nike ad says, "Just do it!"

"Free your mind..."

Do you have a bucket list?

_____

_____

_____

_____

_____

What is your secret bucket list item that you are reluctant to share with others?

_____

_____

_____

_____

_____

_____

Colossians 3:17

Whatever you do in word or deed, do all in the name of the Lord Jesus, giving thanks to God and the Father through him.

CHAPTER EIGHT:

Did I Ever Thank You?

Did I Ever Thank You?

I know it may be a little unconventional to use an entire chapter just to say thank you; but you've done so much for me, and you continue to inspire, motivate and uplift me. Below are all the things I'd like to thank family, friends, associates, medical personnel, and strangers for. This poem is for those of you I know by name and those whose names I'll never know.

Did I Ever Thank You?   © Freda Mays, December 2014

Did I ever thank you for your phone calls
Your texts and beautiful cards
Did I thank you for keeping me on your prayer list
Just knowing this journey would be hard

Did I thank you for the gifts, the FaceBook posts
And all the heart-felt prayers
Did I tell you how thankful I am
Knowing that you even care

Did I ever thank you for the wishful thoughts
On the days I couldn't compete
Or for the day you reached to hug my neck
Because I was broken and could not speak

Thank you for the day you pulled me close
To whisper in my ear with care
Saying to me in a loving voice
Girl, I think it's time for some new hair

Did I thank you for the hot meals
You brought right to my door
Just because you loved me
Just know, I love you more

Thank you for just leaving me be
When you detected I needed my space
Though I know you wanted to hold my hand
And kiss my troubled face

Thank you for the day you told me I was cute
Decked out in jeans from Guess
Although you probably walked away
And said, Lord she's a hot mess!

Did I ever thank you for keeping my secrets
Allowing me to bend your ear
Feeling a little broken at times
Sharing my every fear

Thank you for always setting me straight
Not ever letting me off the hook
Your support is greatly appreciated
Thank you so much for buying this book!

Thank you Momma for your guidance
Though you have your own hills to climb
You still walk in our shadow
Always wanting us to shine

Mom, if I see God before you do
Just pray my soul to keep
Always keep your head up and give your best self
And until then, I will "Save You a Seat"

Last but never least, I thank you God
For saving me over and over again
Thank you Lord for the readers of this book
This is my THANK-YOU, *Amen!*

This chapter is dedicated to all of you who sent cards, called, brought food to me, told me about myself when needed, gave me my space, sent love on Facebook, or texted. Thank you also to my Instagram, Twitter and Facebook followers.

Family First
Love is patient and kind; Love does not envy or boast;
It is not arrogant or rude; It does not insist on its own way;
It is not irritable or resentful; It does not rejoice at wrongdoing;
but rejoices with the truth. Love bears all things. Believes all things;
Hopes all things; Endures all things.
1 Corinthians 13: 4-7:

- Thank you and I love you to my friends and family in my hometown Madison Heights, Lynchburg, Danville and Richmond, Virginia.

- A special thanks to my Scott Zion Baptist Church family & friends in Madison Heights, Va., especially Pastor Russell Gary Lee and his family.

- Thank you to Reverend Terrence Gray and the Saint Mark A.M.E. Church in Orlando Florida. "You are my home away from home."

- Thank you to my family and friends in Covington, Columbus and Atlanta, Georgia; and my Philadelphia family.

- A very special thank you to my Uncle Riley in Richmond, Virginia and my DeShazor family in Danville, Virginia...I love you guys.

- Thank you to all my sisters, brothers and especially my nieces and nephews. THANK YOU is in no way enough when it comes to my mother Shirley Megginson, my rock. "YOU ROCK!"

- Thank you to my sister, Bea Ferguson, for being a rock to Mom and to my baby brother who is battling throat cancer. Though you have your own battles to fight you help fight ours. Keep it moving, girl!

TO MY GOD KIDS: Further your education and
always be kind to each other

Do not be conformed to this world, but be trans-
formed by the renewal of your mind,
by testing you may discern what is the will of God,
what is good and acceptable and perfect.
Roman 12:2

Brandy Jones, Covington, Georgia; Chelsea Bryant, Jacksonville, Florida; Lorna Capri Rodgers, Richmond, Virginia; Quentin Rawls, Madison Heights, Virginia; Teneshia "China" Ferguson, Lynchburg, Virginia; Yazmin Lafleur, St. Paul, Minnesota; Mark Walker Jr. (A.k.a Manny), Marquette, Michigan; Dynym Allison, Tampa, Florida; Frances Torres, Puerto Rico; and Taylor Aberhart, Atlanta, Georgia.

...Continuation of Family

Greater love has no one than this,
someone lay down his life for his friends.
John 15:13

- Thank you Mary Patton, thank you Jennifer Martin and thank you Lennell "Lucy" Shaw. When I think about you guys a song comes to mind that goes like this, "I don't know why Jesus loves me, I don't know why he cares..." I don't know why you ladies love me the way you do, but I am blessed and glad that you do!

- James Flowers, there are no words to express how proud and blessed I am to know you. Thank you for being one of my biggest supporters over the years. Me casa, you casa...always and forever!

- Joni Hawkins, you have been on this journey with me for over 25 years, WOW! You hold a wealth of knowledge that has benefited so many people. But just as Joel Osteen says, IT'S YOUR TIME NOW! Thank you Jo for being an awesome friend, but more importantly, ALWAYS an awesome mother to the twins, Kaleb and Kyle.

- Drew, "I wish you were here right now." Thank you for the best friendship a girl could have. Thank you for sharing your awesome friends with me; and most of all for your trust. Last but not least, if it wasn't for you, I don't know if I would have ever met R. Kelly; thank you "Cover Girl." I Wish...

- Thank you to my other three mommies: I love you the MOSTEST Vera Flowers (Columbus, Georgia); Anita Alston (Raleigh, North Carolina), and Thelma "Tiny" Kelly (Orlando, Florida). I see you too Kathy Flowers!

- Joyce Hinton – Thank you for wanting to pack me up and move me in with you just because you wanted to make sure I would be okay... I love you Sis!

- Thank you to Paris Wilson for the beautiful art produced in this book...Thank you Master P!

- Thank you to my friends and colleagues at Goodwill Industries of Central Florida. A very special thanks to Bill Oakley, CEO/President at Goodwill Industries of Central Florida, for heartfelt words that have had a great impact on my life. I am forever grateful; and to Linda Rimmer, Vice President of Vocational & Community Services at Goodwill Industries of Central Florida, who've been with me on this journey from day one.

- Thank you, Evelyn Benton-Phelan. This project was born because God blessed me and sent you into my path like an angel in disguise. Thank you for loving and supporting me for twenty-something years. Thank you for making all those outfits for me; including the dress for my first Soul Train Awards Show!

- To my two surrogate daughters; Tanisha Williams in Tampa, Florida and Angela Crumitie, Orlando, Florida...I love you as if I birthed you myself!!!

- Thank you to Sharon Fletcher Jones, (no hyphen, no husband - SMILE) for being my designated driver each and every time I've had to go to the emergency room. And for ALL you do to keep me going.

- Neshia White, I never had the opportunity to thank you for something you did for me on this journey that truly impacted my life at that time. I know it's too personal to mention but as the ending of Drew's joke goes, "You know."

- A BIG thank you to my Atlanta brothers – Devyne Stephens and Wayne Stallings for your forever friendship. Another big thank you to, "you Wheezy, for your part in promoting me and this book." And much love to my Miami brother, Mark Anthony, "Surveillance Anthony."

Friends, Confidants and Free's VIPs

*Beloved, let us love one another, for love is from God,
and whoever loves has been born of God and knows God.*
1 John: 7

- Thank you to my attorney and good friend Julee Milhan; you've been a wonderful friend for over twenty years...thank you for ALWAYS being there for me no matter what!!! Thank you to attorneys Gary Greenberg and Michael Moore for your friendship over past twenty years and counting!

- Thank you Ra-feal Blanco of 2Rs Entertainment and Media for believing in and always supporting me. Thank you to my Glam Squad -- Leo, Eric, Nathan, and Natay -- for making me look so beautiful for my photo shoot.

- Thank you to my "top-twenty" girls in Orlando, for being an awesome support system for me – and for each year you took the time out to attend my annual birthday celebration.

- Thank you to Priscilla Hawkins for assisting me in making this book better than it would have been without you.

- Thank you Willie Clark of Clark Media and the Willie Clark Show for teaching me so much about radio and for helping me promote this book. You can tune in to his show every day, especially Saturday mornings at www.clarkmedianetwork.com

- Thank you to Cassandra Paul for your input then, now and always!

  - Thank you to Ariel Sanabria, a former coworker and friend; and an up and coming comedian in Orlando, Florida for assisting me with presenting my first joke.

- Thank you to the staff at MD Anderson, UF Health and Orlando Regional Medical Center for your hospitality, your smiles and for always making me feel as though we are all in this together, especially the staff on 5LP!

- Thank you to my Free's VIPs Teams for assisting me in marketing my book and not accepting a dime in return; and to my facebook, Instagram and twitter followers. I am forever grateful for what you guys do for me. Thanks for the encouraging words, advice and your prayers. I don't take your kindness for granted, and I will pay it forward.

- I want to thank my oncologist for not only always being at the top of her game, but also for always making every patient feel like a friend or family.

- I want to call each person by name and deed, but that would turn into another book. Please just know that I love you from the bottom of my heart. This chapter is dedicated to you, you, and you too, and it's still not enough!

"Free your mind..."

If you died today, who would you regret not thanking?

_____

_____

_____

_____

_____

Please call someone today to thank them for something they've done or said to add good energy to your life. Who will you call?

_____

_____

_____

_____

_____

_____

Colossians 3:17
And whatever you do, whether in word or deed, do it all in the name of the Lord Jesus, giving thanks to God the Father through him.

CHAPTER NINE:
Finding Joy in the Journey

Finding Joy in the Journey

I am dying! But so are you. We could all be two seconds, or two weeks or maybe two years from dying and never know it. But we still have so much to be thankful for.

I am often asked how I stay so positive. I make a conscious choice to live on purpose, and with a purpose – knowing there are things I can control; and things I can't do a darn thing about. So I choose to keep it moving.

No matter your journey, trials, tribulations or triumphs, there is always something to be thankful for; something that will put joy in your heart. Because things can ALWAYS be worse!

Please believe, we were all put on this earth for a reason. And if you believe, then you must also know God has a purpose for your life. I get up each and every morning with so much appreciation and thankfulness. I know that God has given me another chance to bless someone else, and another opportunity to get my own life right.

My attitude about this journey is that every day I wake up still alive (SMILE), I make a conscious choice to be happy. Even in the midst of darkness, I always trust God. People often say, we have everything we need to do whatever we need to do on this earth. I feel the same way about finding joy, if you look hard enough.

Please don't get me wrong. There are days I still may cry; but the good still outweighs the bad. Because it could be worse!

I've always been a positive thinker. So in the past, whenever I heard anyone say, "I'm tired." – I've always asked them, "What does that mean? Does that mean you're giving up? And if so, what does that look like?" However, now I truly understand what being tired feels like. You get tired of constantly being sick, poked, pumped with poison and always feeling pain in one or several areas not only in your body, but also in life.

But, there are millions of people going through something right now. I believe it's important to recognize when you're tired, and to also express that to your support team (friends, family, etc.). But the key to it all is choosing how you want to go through it.

Cancer is not the worst thing that can happen to you. There are people who are going through so much more. I get fatigued, but I also hear other women saying that all the time. My fatigue may be from treatments and someone else's may be from the challenges of being a single mom. As Robin Roberts says, *Everybody's Got Something*. So how are you going to deal?

I've always believed in doing what works for me, and I encourage you to do the same. Learn to recognize your own silent voice, and then learn to follow it. That's exactly what I did in 2008 when I refused chemo, though my friends and family were begging me to take it. I had to listen to my strong silent voice, which I call "my greater is He that is within me" voice. Again, had I taken the treatment at that time, I truly don't know what my fate would have been. In hindsight it still blows my mind that I refused chemo. That's why I always say it wasn't me, it was God!

People often ask me if I have ever gotten angry at any time on this journey. My answer is "No." Who should I be mad at other than myself? Don't get me wrong; I was devastated about having cancer and losing my breast. But I was more thankful to God for saving my life. If you believe God will work all things together for your good, just strengthen your faith. Be bold in your prayers to Him. Then sit back and watch what happens. He will blow your mind to pieces!

I've found a lot of joy in listening to music, comedy and helping others. But the core of my joy has been totally and implicitly trusting God. None of what I've gone through has been a surprise to Him. He knew way before 2008 what my path would be; and had already paved a way for me. That alone gives me much comfort and joy.

Had my life not led to this point, I don't know if I would have met some of my closest friends. Friends I am so thankful for. These are the kinds of friends who don't come along too often.

One Monday morning, a friend called to ask about my weekend. I told her I was so fatigued I had stayed in -- except for a trip to the store because I'd felt dehydrated and had no bottled water. She began crying and said, "Promise me you won't do that anymore. I will drive thirty miles just to get what you need."

Those are the kind of friends I have -- talk about *joy*! She has always told me I am her "mini me." What really blows my mind is, during the writing of this book, she was diagnosed with stomach cancer; and she still continues to worry about and care for me. ["I love you to pieces, Lucy"]

Another friend, who recently moved out of town, texted me one day to say, "I wish I was there to make sure you have everything you need. But since I'm not, I still won't let that stop me." The next day when I got home, I had a big box in front of my door. I opened the box and found a big pack of paper towels, toilet paper, candles, soup, apple juice, grapefruit juice and much more. I still get care packages every eight weeks or so from my girl, Lyn Sutton. ["Thank you Jongelyn."]

This journey can be a financial hardship, whether you are married or single. But when you're single, the road can be a little tougher, especially financially.

A couple of weeks after I was diagnosed, I called my friend Evelyn Benton-Phelan, owner of Evelyn's Creations in the West Oaks Mall in Ocoee, Florida. After Evelyn got over the shock of me being diagnosed with breast cancer, she began to ask how I was doing financially. I told her I would be fine if my COBRA premium wasn't $981.91. Evelyn and I talked for a few more minutes, and then she abruptly said, "Let me call you back." When she called back, she asked me if I was available for a fund raiser event within the next two weeks.

When Evelyn decides she's going to do something, there is no stopping her. She is surely one of the movers and shakers here in Central Florida. Within less than two weeks, Evelyn gathered her Buffalo Soldiers from Georgia, Florida, North Carolina, Alabama, Virginia and other states. The Buffalo Soldiers is one of the largest black motorcycle clubs in the country. More than forty men and women came out specifically to support someone the majority of them had never laid eyes on. They raised more than $1,200 for me.

Their gift enabled me to pay my COBRA insurance for another month. That was an incredible experience for me. Each person either had on pink or had a pink bandanna or pink shirt tied on their motorcycle.

Since breast cancer affects urban communities the most, we did a 10-mile ride; going through mostly urban areas and the President Barack Obama Parkway. That was my first ride on the back of a motorcycle, and it was an awesome experience. As we rode through neighborhoods, people were blowing their horns and shouting encouraging comments. ["Thank you Evelyn. And thank you to all the Buffalo Soldiers who gave of their time, gas and money to assist me."]

I could continue to give you many testimonies about my friends and life on this journey, but I will save that for another book. Because, it really would take an entire book to tell you the stories of how my friends have blessed my life.

As long as I live, I know life is going to happen. I am so very thankful that God has spared my life for a while longer for whatever reason. That alone brings me joy!

I believe every word God has spoken. I also know He will not leave nor forsake me during the toughest times in my life. Some people who have been diagnosed with cancer may feel God has forsaken them. God never said we wouldn't have to go through something to get to something. But He did say He will be there no matter what.

I did get the cancer diagnosis, but believe me when I tell you, God continues to work it all for my good. If you can't find some joy in just knowing that, I don't know what else to tell you. None of us has control over when we exit this world. We only have control over how we choose to live in it.

Cancer is really not the worst thing that can happen in one's life; though it is one of the diseases that's destroying the African American community by killing so many women. Please know that no matter what you have to endure, God is real and He loves you so much.

I will end by saying this: Just give your best self at all times. Find the joy in your own journey; and always keep it moving. Until then, if you get to heaven before I do, save me a seat!

"Free your mind..."

What is your definition of joy?

_____

_____

_____

_____

_____

On your darkest days, where do you find your joy?

_____

_____

_____

_____

_____

_____

Proverbs 17:22
A joyful heart is good medicine, but a crushed spirit dries up the bones.

CHAPTER TEN:
Keep It Moving

Keep It Moving

If you knew anything about my friend Drew, you would know her motto was, "Keep it moving." That was her "It is what it is" attitude about everything in her life. I still hear her saying those words to me: "Keep it moving, Mays" as if she still knows when I need to hear it.

If you're going to beat the turmoil, the trials, and the tribulations in your life, you have to first show up. If you've ever held a leadership position, I'm sure you've had days when you really wanted to call in sick; but felt it was necessary for you to be there on a particular day.

Unfortunately, once you've been diagnosed with cancer, you are forced into the role of leadership on your journey dealing with doctors; and letting loved ones know how to support you. There may be some days you really don't feel like showing up. And some days you just can't.

But on the days God blesses you with the mental, emotional and physical strength, you have to keep it moving. Otherwise, you'll get knocked straight down and out with -- what-ifs, depression, poor self-image, or lack of financial stability.

No one will ever tell you this is an easy journey. But I will tell you that even in the toughest times -- if you just keep it moving by putting one foot in front of the other -- amazing things will start to happen. God said walk and He will walk with you.

When we're at our lowest, there are friends and family who will try to "talk us off the ledge," so to speak. If you're a little hard-headed like I am, at times you have to get in your own face.

Every now and then reality tries to sweep me off my feet. That's when I have a face-to-face with myself. I say, "Come on now, Freda, you said you trust God. Stop acting like you're the first person this has happened to. God will give you whatever you ask for in His name, so suck it up and keep it moving."

On the days you feel as low as you can go, I dare you to get in front of a mirror – look yourself in the eyes – and speak YOUR truth – to the person in mirror.

This exercise has helped me in many areas of my life. Through this process, I've learned some things about myself. I've learned that life really is 10 percent of what happens to me and 90 percent how I deal with it. How I keep it moving.

I've learned I'm a lot stronger than I ever thought. I've learned to appreciate my body much more. I've also learned that people care more than I thought possible. And their actions show me they care.

My life has changed tremendously over the past few years. I can't participate in a lot of things I used to love doing. I can't easily jog, travel, change furniture around, visit my friends or work an eight-hour job. It takes me all day – and sometimes a couple of days -- to clean my house because I have to keep stopping to renew my energy.

So what? I am really happy to still be able to do things for myself -- so I keep it moving.

With each phase of this journey, I become more grateful. The last time I was in the hospital, though I still felt like crap, I was so excited when the doctor said it wasn't my heart or cancer. I was so thankful because whatever it was, there was a remedy for it -- and I could keep it moving.

Most chemotherapy has numerous side effects. Stiff joints are a side effect of the chemotherapy I'm currently getting. But I'm also 55 years old, and I see some people my age who don't have a debilitating disease; yet they're suffering from some of the same ailments.

The past two years have been like an out-of-control hurricane for me. I lost Drew and two more friends in 2012. One of them, Justo Torres, was only 44 years old with a wife and four young kids. The other friend was Billye Love, a.k.a. *Lady Love*. Billye was a popular radio personality at a station in Orlando.

I lost my godmother, who was also my aunt; my mom's sister. Another best friend lost her mother, who was buried on my birthday -- January 24, 2014. And cancer returned to my body in 2012. I'm telling you all this because, through it all, I still choose – to keep it moving.

I've always loved life and get excited to see what the next new day will bring. Sometimes it's good, and at times it's not so great. Either way, it's another opportunity to learn or teach; lead or follow; poop or get the heck off the pot...just keep it moving!

When you are in the fourth stage of any cancer and become very sick, dying may enter your mind more often than it does for the average person. I use to think I was the only one who thought that way. However, recently I heard several other cancer survivors say they have felt the same way. I'm sharing this with you because if you are experiencing the same thing, please know you are not alone. Tomorrow is not promised to any of us; I've seen so many young people die over the last few years.

Choose to live while you're still here. Give yourself the time to feel whatever it is you're feeling, but then get up. If you can't get up physically, get up mentally. The mind is where it all starts anyway. If up until now, you've just been going through the motions and letting life live you instead of you living life – STOP! Live on purpose now!

Everything you touch, everything you do – make it on purpose. Even that piece of furniture that's just been sitting in a storage or a garage for a very long time. Let's just call it a chair. When you bought it, you had a purpose for it. But for whatever reason, you've just let it sit and sit and sit.

At this stage in life nothing should be purposeless. Everything and I mean EVERYTHING should have a purpose. That's the way I see it if it's going to be in my life. Dust off that chair, find the perfect throw pillow for it, and put it in a purposeful place in your life. Now, stand back and take a look at it, admire it, heck, take a sit in it - - but don't sit too long...

All I'm saying is this: *Keep it moving while you can.*

"Free your mind..."

What or who is stopping you from keeping it moving?

_____

_____

_____

_____

_____

What's your secret to keeping it moving?

_____

_____

_____

_____

_____

Philippians 3:12-14

Not I have already obtained this or am already perfect, but I press on to make it my own, because Christ Jesus has made me his own. Brothers, I do not consider I have made it my own. But one thing I do: forgetting what lies behind and straining forward to what lies ahead, I press on toward.

Suggestions, Last Wishes, and My Plea to You
Suggestions
Friends and family are always asking what they can do for me and others in my shoes. Here is a short list of wishes for those surviving cancer. I hope it will be helpful.

- If your friend or loved one is home and you'll be in the vicinity, call to see if you can pick up anything for them. They may say no, because they don't feel well, don't want to get out of bed, put on clothes, or come to the door. Let your friend or loved one know you will leave the item at the door or hang it on the doorknob, if necessary.

- Or, if you know you will be in the area, ask if the person wants to go to the store to get out of the house. Offer to take them.

- Keep as much humor as possible in the day; tell a funny joke.

- Many of us love fresh flowers. I have often bought them for myself; however, I do not like too many plants and flowers around at the same time. It makes me feel like I'm already dead imagining that's what it will probably look like.

- if you come to visit, before you leave, see if there is any trash to be taken out. Offer to take it out when you go. When we are fatigued, any task seems like a chore.

- <u>Do not visit us if you're sick</u> or feel that you're coming down with something. If you have the slightest cough or cold, please stay away. Our immune systems are already compromised, and we are likely to catch any illness you may have.

- This is a tough journey, and we have our individual ways of dealing. Please don't be so quick to judge us for how we cope, and stop comparing us to other people in our shoes. There are many forms of chemo, and every individual body will react in different ways. In most cases, we are doing the best we can.

- At times, our appetite is not good. Stop trying to force us to eat and instead work with us to find out what might work. When I try to force myself to eat, I end up gagging or throwing up because the food tastes like cardboard.

- If you're cooking, call to see if what you're planning to prepare is something the person has a taste for.

My Last Wishes If I Am Incapacitated

- Please keep my feet warm. Due to the treatments, they hurt worse when they're cold.
- If you're going to take pictures or selfies with me, please allow me to keep my dignity and fix me up a little with a nice wig, preferably human hair, earrings, lip gloss, etc.
- Please keep my lips moist at all times.
- Tell me jokes even if you're not sure I can hear you.
- If you're at odds with each other, take it outside my room. I value my time with God, and He is not the author of confusion.
- Talk to me about what you know about God.
- Please do not let me be in pain under any circumstances. Too much morphine makes me itch; if it is administered, please administer Benadryl as well.
- If the doctor comes in to relay more bad news, keep it out of my hearing range, especially if I already know I'm dying.
- I usually won't allow visitors if I'm not feeling very well; however, if you are visiting and you notice I don't feel very well, please shorten your visit.
- Please forgive me if I owe you an apology for something I've done to you or to someone you love.

My Plea to You

Until I was diagnosed with breast cancer, I had no idea African American women <u>die more often</u> from breast cancer than women of other races. Though white women are diagnosed with breast cancer more often than any other race, African American women are diagnosed at a much younger age than white, Native American, and Hispanic women.

I am alarmed, because unless you research it, you may never know. We see many commercials and ads but none shedding light on how much breast cancer affects the African American community.

I was negligent with my health by not getting my recommended mammograms for a couple of years. Why? Because, again, I was not aware that 85 percent of newly diagnosed cases are women who have no history of breast cancer.

I beg you, please follow through on your recommended mammograms; it may be that one of the reasons African American women die more often from breast cancer, is that we are the group that most often <u>fails to get recommended mammogram exams or participate in clinical trials</u>. I promise I will do better if you will. It's going to take a village.

Facts about African American Women and Breast Cancer
All information and statistics were taken from the American Cancer Society website: www.cancer.org

- Breast cancer is the most commonly diagnosed cancer among African American women; similar to the pattern among white women, breast cancer incidence rates among African American women increased rapidly during the 1980s, largely due to increased detection as the use of mammography screening increased.

- Among younger women (less than forty-five years), incidence rates are higher among African Americans than whites. The median age of diagnosis is fifty-seven years for African American women, compared to sixty-two years for white women.

- All women can help reduce their risk of breast cancer by avoiding weight gain and obesity (for postmenopausal breast cancer), engaging in regular physical activity, and minimizing alcohol intake.

- Breast cancer is the second most common cause of cancer death among African American women, surpassed only by lung cancer. An estimated 6,080 deaths from breast cancer are expected to occur among African American women in 2013.

- Factors contribute to higher death rates among African American women include differences in access to and utilization of early detection and treatment, as well as differences in tumor characteristics; however, much of this disparity remains unexplained.

For more information, resources, and statistics, visit:
The American Cancer Society website www.cancer.org

Also check out www.sistersnetworkinc.org

While being committed to increasing local and national attention to the devastating impact breast cancer has in the African American community, to my knowledge, they are the only national African American BREAST CANCER SURVIVORSHIP ORGANIZATION.

To find a list of providers for bras, wigs, and other headgear, ask your treating doctor; and research the resources in your local area. Resources will vary from state to state.

I want to share a little bit about the artist who produced all the artwork for this project; his story and drive is incredible!

Paris L. Wilson is an African American artist known primarily for his extraordinary portraiture and architectural renderings. The award winning illustrator was born with severe birth defects believed to be caused by thalidomide, an experimental drug given to women in the 1950's to relieve menstrual cramps. Born without a left hand, leg, or jawbone, Wilson's right hand is webbed with two smaller than average-sized fingers. At five years old, a nurse at the Hospital for Crippled Children in Richmond, Virginia gave Paris a sketch pad and pencils for Christmas and ignited his passion for drawing. Wilson was in junior high school when someone called him an artist and he believed it. He credits his siblings (a brother and a sister) for inspiring him to "live beyond his prostheses." The self-taught artist continues to dazzle patrons, enthusiasts, and fellow artists with his technique. Using a digital pen and computer or brush strokes on canvas, Wilson creates a multi-dimensional interpretation of his subject within a single composition.

Wilson greatly admires Michelangelo because of his conviction to portray the Gospel through art, Christian Lassiter for his use of vibrant colors, and Thomas Kincaid for "everything." His works include photographic reproductions, blue print and finished structure renderings, conceptual translations, and caricature. Wilson's most recently completed projects include a portrait of R. Kelly and design and architectural renderings for an academic facility in Brevard, Florida. Although he was given a life expectancy of three weeks at birth, Wilson continues to defy the odds.

Visit Paris L. Wilson on Facebook and click on Paris' Photos to view a sampling of his works.

About the Author

What others are saying about the author...

Love notes from Facebook

My dear cousin, you have been a mother to many of your family members, this I know. You don't have to bear a child to be a mom. You have Godchildren and your friends' kids who love and respect you as though you are their mother. You are an amazing person. You are so blessed. You have a good heart and an old soul. Your heart is so good that you would give or help without question. Your soul is so old it goes back to Grandma, praying, giving, listening, and helping others. You are blessed, because you are loved by so many, family, friends, co-workers, associates, and most of all me. I am also an old soul. Love You Always.
Esther Holland

You inspire me so much! I am so proud to be in this circle of pink with you. I'm not going to say my heart is not saddened, but my spirit is going to remain encouraged for you. Keep praying. Keep pressing.
Sheryl Walker (another survivor)

Keep your head up sis. Continue to trust God with your whole life. Leave nothing that is not turned completely over to Him. He's got you and He always will have you. Also, don't let the fear of possibilities cancel the effects of your faith. Believe in no uncertain terms. Unwavering. Without any doubt. Believe He can do anything. ANYTHING. Much love to you and prayers for your success in this, probably your greatest battle. You're up for the challenge because of Whose you are and Who you are in Him!

Raymer Kelly

Freda, God is walking with you through these times and He is so good. Your greatest gifts to your family, friends, and many new Facebook followers are being heard and felt on each update. I would say that your Faith, Love, Strength, and beautiful use of words are being used by God now as He has blessed you over a lifetime with those gifts to minister to us all. It's an understatement to say that 'we all are praying for you' but it is a great testament to know, 'we are all praying with you.' Be Blessed! For the love of Christ!

James Pennix

Praying for you. God already has a plan for you more than what you are expecting you may have to give up your job But Our God will keep you busy doing things... going places you didn't have a chance to do while you were in the work zone but keep on praying.. I know you will be just fine. Yes God Love You More!!

Virginia Mccoy

You have ALWAYS inspired me and NOW I have been diagnosed with stage 2 breast cancer....I now see God put YOU IN M LIFE FOR A REASON!!! Uplifting words and your fight and drive IS WHAT IM TAKING AWAY FROM THIS DIAGNOSIS... AND AS YOU WILL I TOO WILL FIGHT A GOOD FIGHT!!! GOD IS IN CONTROL MY SISTER.

Dee Turner (another survivor)

Author

"FREE"

Freda L. Mays
Entrepreneur, Branding Executive, Author

Gifted with a portfolio of varied roles, Freda L. Mays, also known as "Free," has demonstrated her multifaceted skills in the entertainment industry with a savvy business sense and creative intuitiveness. Through the years, Mays has succeeded in the fields of talent management, marketing and branding, and business consultation; and is now taking on a new role, author.

Her astute understanding of the urban market and business leadership credentials were instrumental in engineering a conglomerate of musical talent that has shone with platinum luster.

Her musical expertise has been pivotal in the multiplatinum success of acts such as the 69 Boyz and the Quad City DJs. As a definitive leader in the business community, she has utilized her leadership skills in the marketplace by assisting in negotiating multimillion-dollar deals with independent and major record labels such as Atlantic Records, Elektra Records, LaFace Records, and So So Def Records.

Mays also oversaw the day-to-day operations for the independent label QuadraSound Records based in Orlando, Florida. In addition, she demonstrated exceptional marketing strategies by placing strong emphasis on street promotions and targeted marketing through aggressive street campaigns, prominent media exposure, and negotiating soundtrack appearances. She also implemented artist development programs to enhance artists' performances and stage personas.

May served as former personal manager of several successful acts that included the 69 Boyz, Quad City DJs, 95 South, RAab, Dis-n-Dat, and the vocal R&B quartet II D Extreme. She has been instrumental in helping most of these acts reach platinum or multiplatinum success.

With her assistance, the 69 Boyz's debut album, *199Quad* went double platinum; boosted by the phenomenal success of the hit single "Tootsee Roll." As a result, she spearheaded the Bass Fest Tour, which introduced "Southern Hip-Hop" to the masses. The first of its kind, the tour featured artists Outkast, 69 Boyz, Quad City DJs, 95 South, and Dis-n-Dat.

She was pivotal in the platinum success of the debut album of the Quad City DJs, and hit singles "C'mon N Ride It (The Train)" and "Space Jam." She also utilized her extensive business connections to afford the acts the opportunity to land on some of the most lucrative soundtracks to date, including *Dr. Dolittle, Dangerous Minds, Blue Streak, High School High, Sunset Park*, and *Space Jam*. The title song on the *Space Jam* soundtrack titled "Space Jam," performed by Quad City DJs, led to a 1998 Grammy nomination for them for Best Dance Song of the Year.

Mays began her music career in street promotions. Her work in street promotions provided her with a great training ground and gave her the motivation and incentive to bring other creative ideas and goals to life. From street promotions to showcases to management to business consulting, Mays has explored all facets of the music industry.

In 2008, Mays was diagnosed with a form of advanced-stage breast cancer. She endured a mastectomy, and after an entire year of chemo and radiation, Mays went into remission in December 2009. Three years later, in February 2012, the cancer returned; but this time it had spread to her lung, which led her into another phase of chemotherapy.

Fast-forward to early 2014. Mays had begun celebrating when her oncologist delivered what appeared to be great news. Her current treatments were working well for her body; and if she received three clear scans in a row, chemotherapy could stop.

With two clear scans already, Mays was not expecting the news the doctor delivered. As fate would have it, when she went in for results from her third scan, in February 2014, the news was not good. She was told the cancer had spread to six other areas in her body, and she would now have to be on treatments indefinitely.

By August 2014, Mays had to give up working full time in order to concentrate on her health. However, this multitalented career woman from Virginia is unstoppable and full of faith.

Connect with the Author

Freda@werdpublishing.com
Facebook: fredamays(author)
Twitter: iamfredamays
Instagram: iamfredamays

MY CONVERSATION WITH GOD

© Freda May, October, 2014

I had a conversation with God
And here is how it went
He first told me that He loves me
And said I was God sent

He said at times I may find myself in tough places
At times I may stumble and fall
He said the only thing I needed to remember
Is on His name to ALWAYS call

I said, Lord help me fathom my situation
I still can't believe I have cancer
It took me a second, but I finally got it
When "Jesus Wept," was His answer

I said, Lord, just continue to strengthen my faith
At times my life lines are so blurred
He told me no matter what, He has my back
And continue to spread His word

He said, continue to tell others
About what I've done for you
Praying they will know within their souls
I will do the same for them too

I ended this conversation by thanking God
For so much mercy, blessings, and grace
I thanked Him for covering me with so much love
While I'm still here taking up space!

May God bless all of you! ALWAYS!